THE ONSEN EXPERIENCE

A Guide to Japan's Hot Spring Sanctuaries

IRIS LAW

This book is a very captivating introduction to the unique onsen resorts and inns across Japan, covering the history and ancient traditions as well as the many types of hot springs that can be found. Hot springs form a fundamental part of the country, and it is important to understand the specifics of an onsen in relation to its local environment, history, and religious background.

Toji ("hot spring therapy") forms the basis of Japanese wellness tourism, and it is starting to attract worldwide attention as part of the wellness movement. I am so pleased that Iris has managed to convey this wellness aspect of the hot springs in her book.

Other countries have begun to study Japanese hot springs, and Japan itself is now attempting to register the onsen as a UNESCO Intangible Cultural Heritage. I want to express my sincere thanks to Iris for capturing the charm of these Japanese hot springs.

-Takuya Fukatsu
Chairman, Minakami Tourism Association,
Gunma Prefecture, Japan

I was curious about Japan and its famous hot springs, but I didn't speak Japanese. I had heard that a friend of mine knew something about them, so I asked her for help. She gave me some pointers, including where to go in Japan — except it wasn't just advice.

This friend was Iris Law. Since then, I've had the great fortune of having Iris guide me across the length of Japan, opening my eyes to the stories behind each onsen ryokan — from its history and its people, to the food served and the water used in the onsen baths.

Let Iris be your guide too. She will help you discover and understand the fascinating world of hot springs, and inspire you to visit and experience them for yourself.

- Gallant Nien, Travel Partner

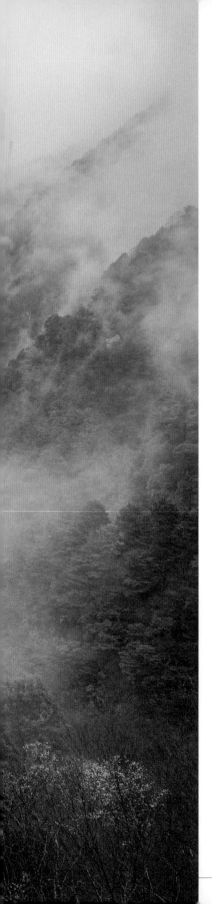

Table of Contents

There is something about the Japanese way of relaxation that I am hopelessly addicted to. Thanks to its distinct volcano-blessed geography, Japan is literally home to thousands of hot springs (that's onsen in Japanese). And naturally, this has given rise to thousands of hot spring inns (or onsen ryokan in Japanese) — most of which are located far away from the bustling cities and hidden instead near oceans, forests, or deep in the mountains.

These sanctuaries proudly promote long-standing Japanese traditions; they offer a place to rejuvenate one's physical and spiritual well-being. Onsen ryokan lodgings offer an incredible combination of well-preserved traditions, immaculate aesthetics, fine hospitality, and delicious local cuisine. And the hot and healing waters that are the stars of the show not only rejuvenate the body but also dissolve away everyday stress and worries.

In this book, I hope to share some useful information on the most breathtaking hot spring inns that I have personally visited over the years, as well as my personal experiences during these visits.

Having stayed at more than 100 ryokan accommodations in Japan thus far, I want to inspire others to discover the rich beauty of Japan's ryokan heritage and onsen culture. A whole range of ryokan offerings is included in this book, from the rustic to the luxurious, and from the centuries-old to the contemporary.

I've focused more on the boutique family-run inns that have been passed on for generations, since each one is unique in style and personality. Many visitors already know to go to a Japanese ryokan to soak in the onsen waters, to eat, and to rest. But the experience would be even more memorable if one could understand and appreciate the history, the inspiring stories, the people, and other behind-the-scenes aspects of an onsen ryokan. This is what I hope to achieve with The Onsen Experience.

It is beyond words to describe how amazing it has been to be able to write this book. I have truly enjoyed every single step of this journey. This whole project would not have been possible without the help of many people, in particular:

My editor Adele Wong and publisher Man Mo Media — my gratitude goes to you for your trust in me and for providing guidance throughout this project. Creative director Mike Hung, your incredible vision made my book come to life.

I am more than thankful to the owners and staff of the ryokan accommodations for their hospitality, and for their help in providing the information I needed, as well as for accepting my invitation to be a part of this book.

Special thanks to Minakami Tourism Association for their assistance and support.

Miya Huang, a big thank you for your marvelous translation work.

Keiko Nishiuchi, thank you so much for your meticulous proofreading efforts.

Neri Ishida, I fell in love with your paintings the first time I saw them. The honor is mine in having your illustrations grace this book.

My sister Heidie Law: thank you for your understanding and for taking care of me. For too many days, I've had to isolate myself and abandon all housework in order to write.

Gallant Nien, I never would have thought of writing this book if not for your encouragement. You have witnessed every step I have taken in working through this project. It means a lot to me to have your company and your tremendous support.

Lastly, thank you Lord for giving me the courage and wisdom to write. May all glory be Yours.

-Iris Law

FIRST, SOME BACKGROUND

The word onsen (温泉) means "hot spring" in Japanese, and there are more than 30,000 natural onsen sources across Japan. These natural hot springs have spawned thousands of onsen ryokan ("hot spring inn") accommodations across the country, offering a relaxing way for guests to unwind. The steamy water baths also contain high levels of minerals that are believed to provide health benefits for the body.

In 1948, the Onsenhou ("Hot Spring Law") came into effect with an official definition of the onsen: a body of natural spring water must contain a critical level of natural minerals and chemicals, and its temperature must be 25 degrees Celsius or above, before it can be labeled as an onsen.

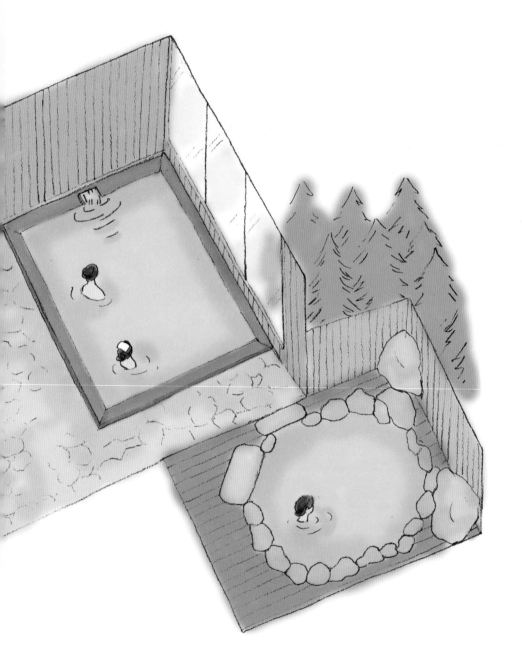

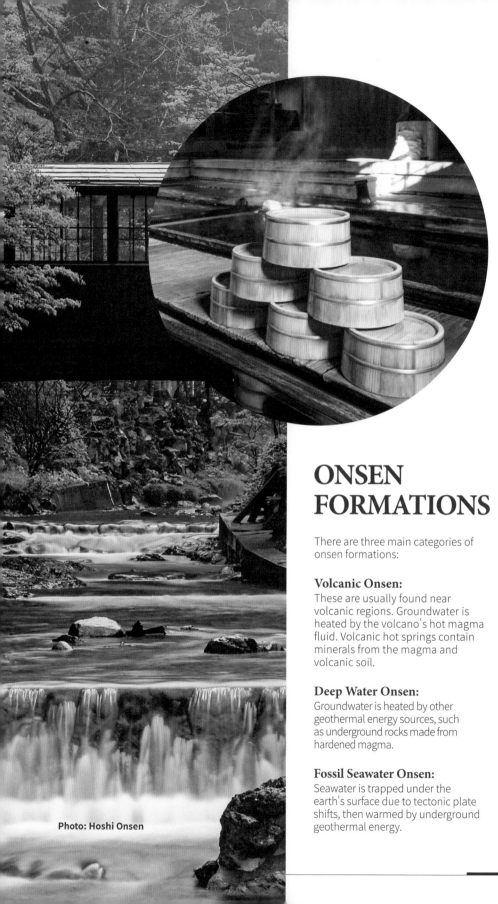

Photo: Hoshi Onsen

ONSEN FORMATIONS

There are three main categories of onsen formations:

Volcanic Onsen:
These are usually found near volcanic regions. Groundwater is heated by the volcano's hot magma fluid. Volcanic hot springs contain minerals from the magma and volcanic soil.

Deep Water Onsen:
Groundwater is heated by other geothermal energy sources, such as underground rocks made from hardened magma.

Fossil Seawater Onsen:
Seawater is trapped under the earth's surface due to tectonic plate shifts, then warmed by underground geothermal energy.

ONSEN TYPES

There are 10 major onsen types in Japan, each containing different mineral properties and boasting different health benefits, all due to differences in the composition, pH, temperature, color, smell, texture and taste of the water.

Information about an onsen is usually posted on the wall of the bathhouse dressing room inside the ryokan.

Onsen Type	Description	Alleged Health Benefits
Simple Spring	The most basic form of hot spring, with the lowest levels of minerals. Slightly alkaline. Clear and odorless.	Helps with recovery from fatigue, nerve pain, insomnia, high blood pressure. Soothes the skin.
Chloride Spring	The most common type of hot spring in Japan. Usually contains sodium and calcium. Clear and odorless.	Helps with recovery from illness, infertility. Alleviates muscle/joint pain, sprains, sensitivity to cold, chronic diseases.
Carbonate / Bicarbonate Spring	There are two sub-types: bicarbonate springs and sodium bicarbonate springs. Clear and odorless.	Alleviates muscle/joint pain. Soothes cuts. Eases chronic skin diseases.
Sulfate Spring	Usually contains sodium, calcium and/or magnesium. Bitter in taste. Varies in color and odor.	Helps with rheumatism, bruises, cuts, burns, high blood pressure, external wounds.
Carbon Dioxide Spring	Rare in Japan. Contains lots of bubbles. Clear and odorless.	Relieves muscle/joint pain, high blood pressure, cuts, sensitivity to cold, menopausal disorders, infertility. Helps lower blood pressure.
Acidic Spring	A stimulating hot spring that causes tingling sensations on the skin. Varies in color and odor.	Helps with chronic skin diseases, diabetes, athlete's foot. Strong sterilizing properties.
Sulfur Spring	Known for its strong "rotten egg" odor. Pale yellow in color.	Relieves high blood pressure, chronic skin diseases, joint pain.
Iron or Copper Spring	High in iron or copper. Water turns from colorless to dark reddish-brown when exposed to oxygen. Odorless, or slightly rusty odor.	Offers relief from anemia, rheumatism, menopausal disorders, chronic eczema.
Radium Spring	Also referred to as Radon Spring or Radioactive Spring. Contains a very low level of radioactive minerals that are said to be beneficial for the body. Rare in Japan.	Relieves high blood pressure, nerve pain, rheumatism, gout.
Aluminum Spring	Colorless and transparent, or a yellowish-brown color with a bitter taste. Strong sterilizing properties. Bitter in taste.	Strong sterilizing properties.

BATHING PROCEDURES

Rinsing:

Before dipping into an onsen, rinse your body first with a few buckets of hot spring water, allowing it to get used to the temperature. Use the bucket provided in the communal bath, and pour water over your feet and all the way up to your upper body. You may also use soap.

First Soak:

After rinsing, enter the hot spring and slowly immerse your body into the water to get acclimated.

Showering:

After soaking for about 5 minutes, get out of the onsen and take a proper shower with soap.

SOME POINTERS

It is important to be respectful when you're at a Japanese onsen. In Japan, it's all about manners. People go to an onsen to relax, recuperate and enjoy themselves, and the expectation is that they can do this in peace.

Here are some guidelines for your next dip:

1. Change into the **yukata** (cotton robe) that is normally placed in the closet of your room. Be sure to wear it with the left side over the right.

2. Bring a small and big bath towel to the **daiyokujo** (大浴場 , "large communal bath"), also usually placed in the closet of your room. Some lodgings have towels available at the communal bath.

3. Keep valuables in your room, or put them in a locker in the changing room if there's one available.

4. The communal baths usually come with gender-specific **datsuijo** (脱衣所) changing rooms. There should be noren fabric curtains displayed at the entrance: red for women, blue for men.

Final Soak:
Re-enter the onsen and soak again, then take a break or get out of the onsen. Showering after the final soak is not recommended, since this will wash away the minerals that have been absorbed into your skin.

Drying:
Wipe away excess water on your body with a small towel before re-entering the changing room. Be mindful to not let water drip all over the floor of the changing room.

Rehydrating:
After soaking in an onsen, make sure to replenish your body and energy levels by drinking lots of water.

5. Most ryokan lodgings alternate their female and male changing rooms at a designated time each day. Follow the color of the noren curtains to enter the right one.

6. Remove your slippers or shoes before entering the changing room.

7. There should be individual lockers or baskets in the changing rooms. Remove your clothes completely and leave them in the basket or locker of your choice.

8. Only the small towel can be taken with you into the bathing area. It can be used for cleaning and for modesty if needed.

9. If you are not 100 percent comfortable being in the nude, use the small towel to cover your body.

ONE MORE THING...
We make use of a lot of native Japanese terms throughout this book, and we usually explain these terms on the first instance their mention. However, when in doubt about a term (that has been bolded), simply search the glossary at the back for the proper definition.

DOS & DON'TS

Don't wash yourself in the onsen bath. Washing should be done in the shower area.

Photographs are prohibited inside the changing room and the bathing areas.

Don't swim or jump into the onsen.

Avoid letting your hair touch the water. If you have long hair, tie it up.

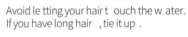

Swimwear is not allowed.

While showering, be mindful not to splash your neighbors.

Keep your towel out of the water, and don't wash and wring your towel in the onsen. Submerging the towel is frowned upon, although you can wear it on your head if you wish.

Avoid speaking loudly while bathing. Treat the bathhouse as a sacred space.

While using mixed-gender baths, respect the opposite gender. Ogling is definitely not a good idea. Some mixed-gender baths have signs that prompt women and men to stay on opposite sides of the bath.

FAQ

Can I cover myself with a towel or wear a swimsuit in a mixed-gender bath?

In some mixed-gender baths, towels or cover-ups are provided by the ryokan. However, in the more traditional mixed-gender baths, nothing can be dipped into the water except your naked body!

How long should I soak for?

Generally, soaking time should be no more than 10 minutes, with a break in between. This can be repeated two to three times. Take a break by sitting up with your heart above the water. Exit immediately if you feel dizzy or unwell.

When is it not a good time to bathe in an onsen?

Immediately after eating or drinking alcohol.

I have tattoos. Can I use the onsen?

Those with tattoos are generally not allowed to enter the communal baths in Japan, but waterproof tattoo bandages can be taped over the tattoos. A small number of inns do allow those with tattoos to enter — it's best to call and check beforehand. Alternatively, stay at a ryokan with a private onsen in the room.

Can I drink the hot spring water?

While some hot spring water is classified as **insen** (飲泉, "potable spring"), you should never drink the water right from the onsen pool, since it might contain disinfectants. Only consume water dispensed from designated spring water taps that are labeled safe to drink.

Can I wear jewelry and accessories in the baths?

Although there are no strict rules regarding the wearing of jewelry and accessories, they may react with the minerals in the spring water and cause damage to your possessions.

Can I keep the towels that were given to me?

The small towel is a gift for the guest. The big towel stays at the ryokan.

ONSEN REGIONS MAP

In this book, we take you through 23 of the most breathtaking onsen ryokan locations across Japan. The ryokan selections are spread across eight different regions.

Kyushu
1. Tenku no Mori, Kagoshima
2. Gajoen, Kagoshima
3. Ishiharaso, Kagoshima
4. Takefue, Kumamoto
5. Kamenoi Bessou, Oita

Chugoku
6. Shouen, Shimane

Shikoku
7. Iya Onsen, Tokushima

Kansai
8. Mikiya, Hyogo
9. Suisen, Kyoto

Chubu
10. Beniya Mukayu, Ishikawa
11. Yumoto Saito, Nagano
12. Satoyama Jujo, Niigata

Kanto
13. Naraya, Gunma
14. Hoshi Onsen, Gunma
15. Tatsumikan, Gunma
16. Bettei Senjuan, Gunma
17. Hatcho no Yu, Tochigi
18. KAI Nikko, Tochigi

Tohoku
19. Meigetsuso, Yamagata
20. Yamado, Iwate
21. Tsuru no Yu, Akita
22. Aoni Onsen, Aomori

Hokkaido
23. Takinoya, Hokkaido

HOKKAIDO

Sapporo

23

22

21

TOHOKU

Sendai

20
19

12

17
16   18
14
13   15

11

KANTO

CHUBU

Tokyo

Nagoya

霧島温泉
天空の森

Tenku no Mori,
Kagoshima Prefecture

THE STORY

One of the most luxurious ryokan offerings in Japan, and a dream vacation spot for locals, Tenku no Mori is a contemporary resort in Kirishima, Kagoshima Prefecture. It is located on a 60-hectare plot of the mountainous Kirishima forest and consists of only five villas of various styles.

Guests begin the extraordinary journey as soon as they step through the discreet entrance, where they are picked up for a buggy ride through the bamboo groves, an organic vegetable terraced farm, the Ishizaka river that runs through the forest, and the highest peak of the resort (aptly named Gateway to the Sky) before being ushered to their rooms.

Instead of simply running his family-owned classic ryokan, the Tajima Honkan, proprietor Tateo Tajima's bold vision led him to build two new ryokan lodgings in Kirishima: Tenku no Mori (天空の森) and Gajoen (雅叙苑). Tenku no Mori became a member of the Relais & Chateaux luxury hotel association in 2016. Gajoen is also featured in this book.

Tajima first started the Tenku no Mori project on his own in 1992, spending the first eight years breaking the land, re-arranging the forest, and drilling for access to underground onsen water. The first villa started running in 2004. The idea behind Tenku no Mori is to create a place where guests can have absolute privacy and feel connected to the skies.

THE DESIGN

At Tenku no Mori, guests can completely detach from their daily worries and revel in the vast and open space that envelopes the ryokan grounds. Each villa is situated far apart from each other, and guests can bathe entirely nude without worrying about their privacy. Guests are encouraged to spend time at the river to read, enjoy a meal, or go fishing. They can also relax under a tree canopy or simply admire the stars at the Gateway to the Sky.

The Tenku no Mori grounds are elevated, floating on top of lush green trees that look down onto the forest canopy underneath. Further away is the Kirishima volcanic mountain range, and at times its smoky eruptions can be seen from the ryokan. Whether it's a sunny day or a foggy afternoon, the views are equally breathtaking.

The villas all feature an open design, using local materials from the original forest. Tajima works directly with the carpenters to create the most unique furniture pieces featuring a tree's original trunks and branches. The units come with glass doors that ensure guests never lose sight of the beautiful surrounds.

By far one of the most expensive accommodations in Japan, Tenku no Mori also offers a more affordable day-stay option to guests. Two of the villas are reserved for day goers: they can use the villa for a four- to six-hour stretch and enjoy the magnificent environment of Tenku no Mori, as well as a fantastic organic picnic lunch and private open-air onsen bath.

THE WATER

The hot spring water of Kirishima originates from its mountains and the Ishizaka river. The water is stored for years under the rich volcanic soil of Kirishima, and is heated by geothermal energy.

This natural spring water is pumped from 60 meters underground to the villas at Tenku no Mori. Each villa comes with its own **rotenburo** (open-air onsen pool), which sits atop a wide wooden outdoor deck that offers unobstructed panoramic views of the surrounding scenery. The slightly brownish water is high in hydrogen carbonate, which is said to be soothing for the skin and effective against skin inflammations.

THE CUISINE

Food at Tenku no Mori is special — the meals are simple and full of flavors, made from the freshest ingredients from the site-owned organic vegetable and chicken farms. Unlike most Japanese inns, Tenku no Mori does not serve **kaiseki** meals, but more western-style dishes like green salads, freshly baked breads with homemade marmalade and wild honey, and pan-seared free-range chicken or beef. Lunch can be enjoyed at the villa's open-air deck, and dinner can be had at the restaurant.

THE TAKEAWAY

Having had the honor of meeting with owner Tajima, I found him to be an admirable, funny and energetic man. Now in his 70s, he has dedicated himself entirely to building a resort to help people find pure happiness and leisure. It is impressive that he is still very hands-on with many things, from paving the roads to fixing the furniture.

Tenku no Mori is a magical place: the enormous grounds offer absolute privacy and gives me a sense of liberation. I feel so strongly connected to the beautiful natural environment. Staying at this extraordinary resort is a once-in-a-lifetime experience, even though it's a pricey one.

Tenku no Mori
天空の森

Address
3389 Shukukubota, Makizono, Kirishima, Kagoshima Prefecture, 899-6507 | +81 995-76-0777

Website
www.tenku-jp.com

Getting Here
Convenient. Drive from Kagoshima Airport (15min). Tenku no Mori can also arrange a taxi for guests to/ from airport (reserve in advance).

Price Range / Rooms
High-end. Contemporary detached villas.

ONSEN WATER

Type: Carbonate Spring (with sodium, calcium, magnesium elements)

Color and Odor: Slightly rusty; odorless

pH: 6.5

Gensen Kakenagashi: Yes

Filtered and Circulated: No

Temperature at Source: 57.6°C

Temperature at Bath: 40°C to 43°C

Wasure no Sato Gajoen,
Kagoshima Prefecture

霧島妙見温泉

忘れの里 雅叙苑

THE STORY

Nestled at the foot of Mount Kirishima, Wasure no Sato Gajoen is a ryokan in the hot spring town of Myoken Onsen. This traditional boutique Japanese ryokan aims to provide a farm-stay experience, with its charming thatched roof huts and free-roaming chickens. It offers a chance for guests to relive a style of Japanese village life that has long been forgotten. Wasure no Sato means "the forgotten village", after all.

Established by Tateo Tajima, owner of Tenku no Mori, Gajoen is run by Tajima's wife, Etuko Tajima, who is the designated **okami** (ryokan service manager, typically a female and a family member). The couple worked side by side together to successfully create this quintessential countryside ryokan, which became a member of the Relais & Chateaux in 2015.

THE DESIGN

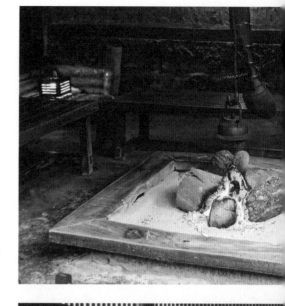

The ryokan consists of rustic farmhouses, complete with roofs made from dried straw. These gorgeous rural cottages have been uprooted and relocated to the current address behind the Amorigawa River, inside a dense deciduous forest. The thatched rooftops peeking through the trees make for quite the scene.

The 10 rooms at Gajoen are of traditional Japanese design, with wooden furnishings, a **tatami**-lined floor, high ceilings, and wooden-framed paper sliding doors. **Kotatsu** (heated low tables with blankets attached) allow you to keep your legs warm during the chilly winter months. Each room is different, and most rooms come with a semi-outdoor private onsen. The Keyaki, Sakura and Momiji Beni are the most popular rooms — they are more spacious and come with a stone onsen bath, a den, and a balcony.

THE WATER

Many visitors travel to the Myoken Onsen area for its healing waters, believed to be highly therapeutic and particularly good for skin problems. The water at Gajoen is piped from the hot spring |sources in Myoken Onsen, and the baths are all **gensen kakenagashi** (源泉かけ流し), or completely from the source.

The water is slightly rusty in color, a result of its rich, oxidized mineral content. There are three public onsen sections available for guests' private use. Takeru Yu (建湯) consists of two large onsen pools, hollowed out of a massive 20-ton rock by Tateo Tajima himself. The water contains high levels of sodium, calcium and magnesium, drawn from the thermal wells underground and heated by the robust volcanic activity of Mount Kirishima. Utase Yu (うたせ湯) consists of two different types of spring-source water; and Ramune Yu (ラムネ湯) is a bubbly carbon dioxide spring that is considered rare in Japan. The temperature of these baths hovers around 41 degrees Celsius.

Gajoen's in-room aqua baths also use the same therapeutic warm waters from Myoken Onsen.

THE CUISINE

The food at Gajoen is a series of simple village dishes, showcasing the richness of the organically grown ingredients from the on-site vegetable and chicken farms. Guests are served nutritious homegrown food for dinner and breakfast at the ryokan restaurant, Ichou no Ma. The neatly arranged utensils are made from raw materials found in the garden, and the menus come with pictures and descriptions, hand-drawn and handwritten by the staff. An English menu is also available for foreign guests.

Food is cooked in a charming old-fashioned open kitchen outside the restaurant, which comes with a traditional wood furnace. The feast starts with an appetizing umeshu (plum wine), slightly seared farm chicken sashimi, and an organic vegetable salad. This is followed by hot dishes that are unique to the region, including a hearty sweet-potato-flour-dumpling soup called dangojiru; boiled Kurobuta pork from Kagoshima farm; miso-marinated vegetables; grilled fish; wild leaf tempura; and soy milk pudding.

At Gajoen, daily breakfast preparations begin before dawn. When the rooster crows and the fragrance of charcoal and food waft into the guest rooms, that's your cue to wake up and indulge in an elaborate morning banquet.

ONSEN WATER

Type: Carbonate Spring (with sodium, calcium, magnesium elements); Carbon Dioxide Spring

Color and Odor: Slightly rusty; odorless

pH: 6.6

Gensen Kakenagashi: Yes

Filtered and Circulated: No

Temperature at Source: 54°C

Temperature at Bath: 41°C

THE TAKEAWAY

There is something about Gajoen that makes me want to revisit it time and time again. Every time I check in, I'm so happy to see Mr. and Mrs. Tajima, who would warmly welcome my return. Perhaps it's the earthly comforts of the countryside setting that make me feel deeply rested here. The laid-back village life helps me to slow down, and to appreciate small details that I normally wouldn't notice. The Keyaki room is my favorite — I can have a good view of Gajoen village from the balcony, at its elevated location. It's most delightful to be able to spend a lazy afternoon reading a book on the daybed in the cozy den. At night, I also enjoy sitting by the hearth near the reception, where a traditional alcoholic beverage called kappo-zake is served free of charge, and other guests can be found for casual conversation.

Wasure no Sato Gajoen
忘れの里 雅叙苑

Address
4230 Shukukubota, Makizono, Kirishima, Kagoshima Prefecture, 899-6507 | +81 995-77-2114

Website
www.gajoen.jp

Getting Here
Convenient. Drive from Kagoshima Airport (15min). Gajoen can arrange a taxi for guests to/from airport (reserve in advance).

Price Range / Rooms
Mid-range. Traditional Japanese style.

Myoken Ishiharaso, Kagoshima Prefecture

妙見温泉

妙見石原荘

THE STORY

Situated at the base of the active volcanoes of Mount Kirishima in Kagoshima Prefecture, Myoken Ishiharaso is a luxurious ryokan offering a very Japanese style of relaxation. It is reputable for its fine **kaiseki** meals, authentic hot springs and heartwarming hospitality.

Ishiharaso is a boutique family-run ryokan owned by the Ishihara family, with only 15 rooms available to ensure the best of guest experiences. The story of Ishiharaso began in 1966, when the founder established the ryokan in one lone stone building. He transported stones from an 80-year-old rice storage warehouse in the city to the ryokan's current address. The Ishikura (石蔵) stone house is still in use today, a reminder of Ishiharaso's simpler past. As the number of guests grew over the years, new buildings were added to cater to the increased demands of customers. Ishiharaso is currently managed by second-generation owner Daisuke Ishihara.

After a relaxing scenic drive that passes through rivers and lush greenery, you will be warmly greeted by Ishiharaso's staff and Lobu the cat. Lobu found his way to the inn's foot bath one day in 2006 — and he's become the ryokan's mascot ever since. He is quite chilled out, and usually likes hanging out at some of the founder's favorite spots.

There are a few staff members at Ishiharaso who can converse in multiple languages, including English, French and Chinese. Be sure to chat them up — you might learn an interesting story or two!

THE DESIGN

Each room at Ishiharaso was designed to resemble a small Japanese tea house. The traditional interiors offer comfort and relaxation, with bamboo **tatami** flooring and **washi** paper sliding doors. The more luxurious rooms are located at the Ishikura, with private baths carrying authentic onsen water that feeds into the pool. Most of the rest of the guest rooms are located in the Honkan (本館 , main building). Some rooms face the Amori River; in the autumn the color-changing trees around the river make for a particularly stunning view.

THE WATER

Myoken Onsen hot spring town, where Ishiharaso is situated, features onsen water that is a mixture of aged underground mountain and river water.

The water is slightly brownish in color and rich in magnesium, calcium and potassium; it flows as quickly as 300 liters per minute at the source. To preserve the authenticity of the onsen water, Ishiharaso's bath pools are built in close proximity to the sources. The onsen experts at Ishiharaso also use a heat regenerator to adjust the temperature of the water from up to 60 degrees Celsius at the source to around 40 to 42 degrees Celsius.

Muku no Ki (椋の木) is a mixed gender **rotenburo** that sits right in front of the Amori River. The water in this bath is high in carbon dioxide, which is said to help relieve high blood pressure and heal certain skin conditions, among other health benefits.

Nanami no Yu (七実の湯) and Mutsumi no Yu (睦実の湯) are the other two open-air baths with a view of the river that can be reserved for private use. Alternatively, guests can also bathe at the indoor gender-separated communal bath, Amoriden (天降殿), which provides shelter from the rain and cold weather.

THE CUISINE

Dining at Ishiharaso is an exquisite and memorable experience. Meals are served at the Ishikura restaurant. Head chef Oomori is a gourmet artisan, presenting traditional Japanese delicacies that are not only delightful on the palate, but also works of art. Every month, he would decide on the menu with the ryokan's **okami**. During springtime, freshly harvested young bamboo is served.

The restaurant's decor is a flawless blend of retro and contemporary design. Pieces of antique kitchenware, ceramic and glassware are stacked up to form dividers for semi-private rooms. Guests would not be seated at the same table twice during their stay.

To enhance the dining experience, Ishiharaso has a fine collection of western wines, **nihonshu** (aka sake) and shochu, Kyushu region's most famous liquor. Shochu is made purely from sweet potato and can be served straight or with ice. It's best to appreciate this local specialty in a locally made glassware called Satsuma kiriko, which involves intricate craftsmanship that dates back to the Edo Period.

ONSEN WATER

Type: Bicarbonate Spring (with sodium, calcium, magnesium elements)

Color and Odor: Slightly brown; odorless

pH: 6.4

Gensen Kakenagashi: Yes

Filtered and Circulated: No

Temperature at Source: 55°C to 60°C

Temperature at Bath: 40°C to 42°C

Myoken Ishiharaso
妙見石原荘

Address
4376 Kareigawa, Hayato,
Kirishima, Kagoshima Prefecture,
899-5113 | +81 995-77-2111

Website
www.m-ishiharaso.com

Getting Here
Convenient. Drive from Kagoshima
Airport (15min). Ishiharaso can
arrange taxi to/from airport.

Price Range / Rooms
High-end. Traditional
Japanese style.

THE TAKEAWAY

Ishiharaso has it all — it's a
ryokan with the best water, food,
accommodations, and people.
It is a ryokan that I visit every year.
I am always impressed by the staff's
meticulous yet un-intrusive attention
on the guests.

I love to soak in the Muku no Ki
rotenburo at night, when it's very
quiet, since it's a little far and a bit
hard to reach. Rarely would I see
anyone in the mixed-gender bath at
this time, so I wouldn't even need
a towel for modesty. I enjoy the
tranquil atmosphere at night, while
listening to the buzzing cicadas and
gazing at the starry skies.

Takefue, Kumamoto Prefecture

黒川温泉
竹ふえ

THE STORY

Quietly tucked among a 32-acre majestic bamboo forest in Shirakawa village, which is situated in Kumamoto Prefecture right next to the popular Kurokawa Onsen town, Takefue is a top-notch ryokan by every measure.

About a two-hour drive from the Fukuoka Airport, Takefue is far removed from the urban bustle and has been offering luxurious retreats for visitors since 1999. Take ("bamboo") has always been regarded by the Japanese as a sacred plant and one that symbolizes purity, strength and prosperity.

Takefue's team of professionally trained staff provides hospitality services that are above and beyond. The serene bamboo grove before the entrance marks the beginning of the journey. Guests are warmly welcomed by friendly staff and treated with welcome sweets and drinks in the room.

THE DESIGN

Each of the 12 lodges at the property is a harmonious blend of contemporary and traditional Japanese design. The rooms come with floor-to-ceiling windows to take advantage of the surrounding bamboo-lined scenery.

The furniture in each room is made from high-quality wood with distinct bamboo finishings, and accompanied by equally luxurious amenities. The English-speaking staff ensures that foreign guests can be at ease throughout their stay.

THE WATER

Takefue is blessed with a number of pure water sources in the area. The water from Shirakawa village is considered one of the top potable water sources in Japan. Active volcano Aso's historical eruptions helped to form layers of rock underground that serve as natural water filters. The living water here contains high levels of oxygen and active minerals, and is crisp and lacking in impurities — not to mention delicious.

The hot spring water and the unique bamboo-filled environment at Takefue all help to make bathing here an unforgettable experience. Each

lodge features an in-room private onsen with a view of the bamboo forest, where you can bathe for as long as you wish. There are also three **kashikiriburo** (貸切風呂 , open-air bath that can be reserved) options here.

The slightly cloudy and yellowish onsen water contains high levels of metasilicate, chorine, sulfate and hydrogen carbonate, said to help beautify and moisturize the skin as well as promote collagen formation, among myriad other benefits. The temperature of the spring at the source is about 68 degrees Celsius, which is too hot for bathing. To maintain the

authenticity of the water, Takefue has adopted a method of controlling the volume of the water piped into the onsen pools in order to cool down the water without using an extra water source. Water temperature is maintained at a comfortable level of 41 to 43 degrees Celsius, depending on the season.

Chikurin no Yu (竹林の湯) is the biggest of the three **rotenburo** baths, and it sits inside the large bamboo grove at the top of the inn. The stone-made pool is big in size and is partly covered by a thatched-roof shelter. Guests are allocated specific times of the day for

private enjoyment. The extraordinary Chikurin **rotenburo** is particularly beautiful at night, under soft lighting that is projected onto the bamboo forest. The scene is romantic, tranquil, and absolutely breathtaking. Spending time here does miracles for the soul.

The Oku no Yu (奥の湯) and Dokutsu Rotenburo (洞窟露天風呂) are the other two open-air baths that are available for reservation for private use.

THE CUISINE

At Takefue, supper and breakfast are served in the room, allowing guests to spend time with their friends and family in a private space. The property was built on a piece of inclined land, without any structural alterations to the natural landscape. Food is delivered via the staff physically climbing up and down plenty of stairs. This type of service definitely involves more effort and higher costs, but it's also what distinguishes Takefue's hospitality from others'.

The head chef decides on the menu every month, mostly using local Kumamoto produce. Dinner is a succession of multi-course **kaiseki** dishes, beginning with an aperitif and a sakizuke (appetizer), followed by a hassun (second course) which usually sets the theme of the dinner and features beautifully arranged seasonal produce on a big bamboo plate. A few outstanding dishes include the fresh sashimi; the squid and bamboo clear soup; the light and crisp tempura and the grilled wagyu beef platter. Every plate is artistically presented and is pleasing to the eyes as well as taste buds.

THE TAKEAWAY

During my stay, I headed back to my room (the Takekiri) after dinner to spend some quiet moments lying on the **tatami** floor and admiring the bamboo forest through the windows. A breeze of pure and fragrant air wafted through, and my ears took delight in the gentle sound of the nearby waterfall and the swishing of the forest leaves. It was truly a healing of the mind for me.

Takefue's biggest **rotenburo**, Chikurin no Yu, is one of my favorite onsen spots of all. How surreal it was to immerse myself into the enormous onsen pool at night, surrounded by an illuminated bamboo grove that spread across the forest. I have the luxury of enjoying this beautiful ryokan because of the owner's respect for the environment. The original bamboo terrain is intact.

Upon departure, I received as souvenirs a bottle of Japanese sake, some fine sake ware, and a framed photograph that was taken during dinner. These additional thoughtful touches made my stay at Takefue even more exceptional.

Takefue
竹ふえ

Address
5725-1 Manganji,
Minamioguni,
Aso, Kumamoto Prefecture,
869-2402 | +81 570-064-559

Website
www.takefue.com

Getting Here
Convenient. Drive from Fukuoka Airport (2.5hrs). There are buses run by Nishitetsu company, from Fukuoka Airport and Hakata Station to Kurokawa Onsen bus station. Takefue provides complimentary car pick-up at the Kurokawa Onsen bus station.

Price Range / Rooms
High-end. Contemporary Japanese and western style.

ONSEN WATER

Type: A combination of Chloride, Carbonated and Sulfate Springs (with sodium elements)

Color and Odor: Slightly cloudy, yellowish; odorless

pH: 6.6

Gensen Kakenagashi: Yes

Filtered and Circulated: No

Temperature at Source: 68°C

Temperature at Bath: 41°C to 43°C

Kamenoi Bessou, Oita Prefecture

由布院温泉

亀の井別荘

THE STORY

Kamenoi Bessou is a highly regarded ryokan in the popular Yufuin Onsen resort town of Oita Prefecture in the Kyushu region. It is located in a tranquil spot at the basin of the twin-peaked Mount Yufu.

Pass through the bustling shop-filled streets of Yunotsuba before arriving at a quiet neighborhood near Kinrin Lake, where Kamenoi Bessou resides. The lake effectively insulates the ryokan from the town's hustle and bustle, and you'll find much calmness once you step through the thatched roof entrance gate.

Yufuin Onsen has a long history that dates back to the Kamakura Period in the 11th and 12th centuries, but its deserted mountain location prevented its popularity. It only started to become a well-known onsen town when Kentaro Nakaya (the third-generation owner of Kamenoi Bessou), along with several ryokan owners in Yufuin, made significant developments to the town in the 1970s.

Kamenoi Bessou was started by the merchants Kumawachi Aburaya and Mijiro Nakaya (grandfather of Kentaro Nakaya) in 1912. There was only one thatched roof cottage at the time that could cater to exactly one group of guests per day.

Kentaro Nakaya was a film director in Tokyo in his early years, and returned to Yufuin in 1962 to inherit Kamenoi Bessou at the age of 28. He and a few other ryokan owners started a number of development projects to help boost tourism in the region. Nakaya also studied town planning on his own, and learned about the concept of health resorts on his visits to southern Germany, which he subsequently brought back to Yufuin. Today, the area attracts more than 300,000 visitors annually.

Nakaya is now in his twilight years, and has passed the management of Kamenoi Bessou onto his eldest son Taro Nakaya.

THE DESIGN

Kamenoi Bessou was created based on the concept of aramahoshiki nichijo, meaning the ideal way of living everyday life. The ryokan is a harmonious blend of traditional and modern Japanese design, paired with elegant architecture. Historic elements like the thatched roofs and gorgeous wooden beams have been carefully preserved. The refurbished dark wood interiors offer a warm and relaxing environment.

The ryokan consists of 14 cottages and six rooms in the main building, which sits inside a 30,000-square-meter primordial forest. Each sound-proof guest room has a different design, and some rooms come with an onsen pool for private use.

THE WATER

There is an abundant supply of hot spring water at Yufuin, thanks to the geothermal underground activity of active volcano Mount Yufu nearby. The water here is clear and soft, and said to be soothing for the skin as well as to help ease muscular and arthritic pains, among other health benefits. The onsen water at Kamenoi Bessou are direct from the source and piped into the gender-separated indoor and outdoor communal baths.

The water is around 50 degrees Celsius at the source, gradually cooled down to around 42 to 43 degrees Celsius. The indoor stone bath is large in size, with a timber-framed conical glass rooftop supported by a huge tree trunk. The bath house is surrounded by large floor-to-ceiling windows. This remarkable design allows the garden's seasonal views to be appreciated under different weather conditions. Dipping in the outdoor cypress bath pool is also a nice treat.

THE CUISINE

Head Chef Matsuura creates outstanding dishes at Kamenoi Bessou, making use of local and seasonal ingredients. Artfully plated dishes are presented in sequence either at the restaurant or in the guest rooms, and each dish is carefully explained by the staff. Some notable dishes include the charcoal-grilled Bungo beef (wagyu raised in Oita prefecture) and free-range local chicken stew, both signature dishes of Yufuin. Chef Matsuura and his team spend hours or even days to prepare the feast. The dining experience can also be enhanced by pairing the meal with the restaurant's selection of western wines or Japanese sake.

Be sure to save some room for after-dinner drinks at Bar Yamaneko. This two-story speakeasy was a sake cellar more than 250 years ago; now it's been tastefully refurbished and features classic wooden beams and stained glass windows. The mood is tranquil and romantic, and time stands still as you admire the beautiful garden scenery of Japanese maples and cherry blossoms outside. During the day, the bar converts to a café called Tea House Tenjo Sajiki, which serves locally roasted coffee, tea and desserts.

THE TAKEAWAY

It was spring time when I visited Kamenoi Bessou. I got to celebrate hanami, or the art of viewing sakura (cherry blossoms) in full bloom.

There is something divine about the sakura — it is a symbol of how beautiful life can be, but it also reminds us of how fragile life is. As I got myself seated comfortably at a garden-facing table at Bar Yamaneko after dinner, I was overwhelmed by the beauty of the illuminated pink clusters in the garden. In that magical moment, I reflected on how important it is to cherish opportunities in our lives, and to live boldly.

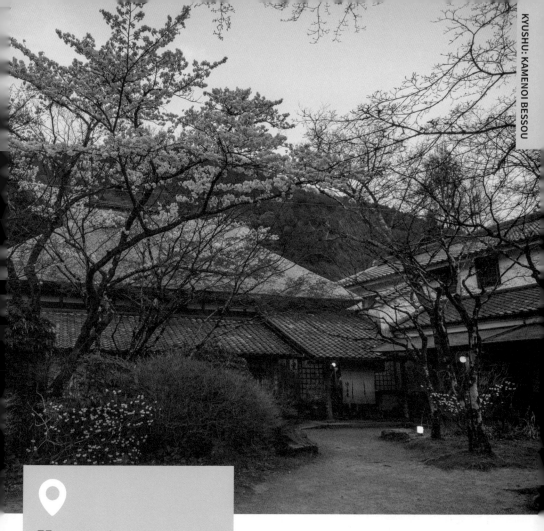

Kamenoi Bessou
亀の井別荘

Address
2633-1 Kawakami, Yufuin, Yufu, Oita Prefecture, 879-5102 | +81 977-84-3166

Website
www.kamenoi-bessou.jp

Getting Here
Convenient. From Fukuoka Airport, take the express bus to arrive at the Yufuin Station Bus Center (100min). Take taxi from bus center (7min).

Price Range / Rooms
High-end. Traditional Japanese style.

ONSEN WATER

Type: Simple Spring

Color and Odor: Clear; odorless

pH: 8.3

Gensen Kakenagashi: Yes

Filtered and Circulated: No

Temperature at Source: 50°C

Temperature at Bath: 42°C

Shouen, Shimane Prefecture

松園 湯の川温泉

THE STORY

The highly spiritual city of Izumo, known as the Land of Gods and the birthplace of ancient Japan, serves as the backdrop for numerous Japanese myths in the book of Kojiki: Japan's oldest history book, based on legends and folklore. The ancient city sits near the coastline of the Sea of Japan in Shimane Prefecture, Chugoku. The history of Izumo stretches back to even before the establishment of the more well-known ancient capitals of Nara and Kyoto. Bronze ware artifacts unearthed from the grounds have revealed its historical existence and importance.

Izumo is also where the oldest and most significant of all Shinto shrines, the Izumo Taisha, is located. The massive shrine features stunning architecture, and hosts ceremonies and a series of rituals to welcome the Kami (gods) from across the country every October.

Inspired by the Japanese mythical stories and legends of Izumo, Shouen is a small family-run, Iron Age-style ryokan situated in Yunokawa Onsen, created by proprietor Takashi Kitawaki. For more than 50 years, the modest owner was committed to building his dream ryokan.

With limited assistance from only a handful of staff members, Shouen is not a ryokan with polished and attentive service; instead, guests can expect casual and wholehearted hospitality here.

THE DESIGN

The main building is a simple two-story concrete structure, but don't be mistaken by the not-too-attractive exterior. You'll find interesting old-world Yayoi-period decor inside the building, such as a distinctive earthen wall assembled with large pieces of round-cornered bricks, and wall paintings depicting life in the Bronze Age, hand-painted by Kitawaki himself.

The traditional Japanese **tatami**-matted rooms in the main building have been nicely refurbished. To enhance the vibe of ancient Izumo, the Kamiyo no Miyadono（神代の宮殿）and Uyatsube（宇夜都弁）lodges opposite the main building

are meant to mimic 2,000-year-old prehistoric dwellings. Both village houses are elevated from the ground, supported by wooden posts, and have ladders to reach the raised entrance.

Kamiyo no Miyadono is a spacious and luxurious Japanese-style **tatami**-matted suite with gleaming wooden beams; while Uyatsube is a replica of a storage warehouse in the Yayoi period featuring rough earthen walls, a sloping straw ceiling, and slanted wooden poles. The rooms are equipped with either futons or western-style beds and modern amenities.

THE WATER

Yunokawa Onsen is a coveted Bijin no Yu (美人の湯, "onsen for beautiful women"), due to the water's alleged beautifying effect. The alkaline water is clear and odorless, and its softening effect on the skin makes it particularly popular among women. Shouen is blessed with Yunokawa's abundant supply of high-quality spring water flowing continuously into the indoor and outdoor onsen bath tubs.

Guests staying at the two special lodgings have access to the bathhouses Magatama no Yu (勾玉の湯) and Takeru no Yu (健の湯) for more private pampering. It's worth mentioning that the bathhouses as well as the special Uyatsube lodge were given an Excellence Award by The Japan Institute of Architecture in Chugoku region.

There are also two gender-separated communal baths in the main building, but these baths are offered to day-trippers until 8pm every evening, so a reservation with the front desk for an after-dinner soak is recommended.

THE CUISINE

Dining at Shouen is different — you'll
have the opportunity to savor the
distinct flavors of ancient Izumo
here. There may be few dinner sets
to choose from, including a standard
kaiseki menu, but it's fun to try the
Yayoi and Jomon period-themed
courses. Kitawaki and his brother
Yuho Kitawaki, who is the main chef
at Shouen, are the masterminds
behind the thoughtfully composed
menu.

The Yayoi course is a primitive feast
featuring 40 to 50 kinds of ingredients
sourced from local fishermen and
farmers. Most dishes are served cold,
with few hot ones brought to the
table during dinner, and bronze ware
and russet-colored clay ware are
used to add to the prehistoric feel.
The food is delicious, from the rice
balls made with three kinds of grains
to grilled wild boar and homemade
cheese based on ancient recipes.

THE TAKEAWAY

Curious to experience a ryokan in an ancient
setting, I chose to stay at the special Uyatsube
lodge. I felt like I was traveling back in time and
found myself standing in this dimly lit earth-
toned old farmhouse, surrounded by prehistoric
figurative hand-drawings on the walls.

For every dish on the menu, Kitawaki-san gave
a detailed explanation on the food's origin and
cooking method, along with precise eating
instructions. I was amazed by how much
he knows about Izumo. Staying at Shouen
was perhaps one of the most special ryokan
experiences I have ever had.

Izumo is a special destination to travel to, with
interesting historical sightseeing spots and some
incredible natural landscapes to explore. A visit
to the Izumo Taisha is a full-day affair, and for a
more in-depth experience, the Shimane Museum
of Ancient Izumo next to the Izumo Taisha
features exhibits on the region's mythology,
evolution and archeological discoveries.

ONSEN WATER

Type: A combination of Sulfate and Chloride Springs (with sodium, calcium elements)

Color and Odor: Clear; odorless

pH: 8.4

Gensen Kakenagashi: Yes

Filtered and Circulated: No

Temperature at Source: 50.5°C

Temperature at Bath: 42°C to 45°C

Shouen
松園

Address
1683-5 Hikawacho Gakuto, Izumo, Shimane Prefecture, 699-0501 | +81 853-72-0024

Website
www.shouen.jp

Getting Here
Convenient. By train: From Shin-Osaka Station, take the Tokado Sanyo Shinkansen to Okayama station (45min), and transfer to the Yakumo Limited Express Izumoshi to Yasugi Station. Take JR San-in Line to Shobara Station. Walk to Shouen (5min). By air: Fly from Tokyo Haneda Airport to Izumo Airport (1hr30min), then take taxi from Izumo Airport to Shouen (5min).

Price Range / Rooms
Mid-range. Traditional Japanese style.

Wanoyado Hotel Iya Onsen, Tokushima Prefecture

祖谷温泉

和の宿ホテル祖谷温泉

Photo: Iya Onsen

THE STORY

Recognized as one of Japan's most secluded sites, Iya Valley lies in the mountainous part of Tokushima Prefecture in Shikoku region. Because it is not too easy to access, the area remains mostly unspoiled.

Iya is often referred to as the "lost paradise" or "hidden valley", after the book "Lost Japan" by American writer Alex Kerr. Old tales and legends refer to the ancestors of Iya as warriors who fled to the secret valley in the 12th century, adding to the area's mysterious and enchanting aura.

One of Iya's most significant historical landmarks is the Kazurabashi bridge, the largest of three surviving suspension bridges in Iya. Walking across this primitive vine bridge is a nerve-wracking experience. Nearby are the narrow rocky canyons of the Oboke gorge and the untamed Yoshino River.

Situated on a steep hill and hidden in the pristine valley landscape is the Wanoyado Hotel Iya Onsen (or simply Hotel Iya Onsen). The drive up the deep V-shaped gorge towards the ryokan is quite a scenic adventure, winding through a very narrow mountainous road and passing by Iya's iconic Peeing Boy statue at the edge of the cliff along the way.

Hotel Iya Onsen was first opened in 1972, and is most well-known for its riverside, open-air hot spring bath at the bottom of the valley, accessible only by the hotel's cable car. There is no lack of visitors to Hotel Iya Onsen, both local and international, despite its secluded location.

Yoshihiro Ueda is the current proprietor; he took over management of the ryokan in 2001, and describes Iya's charming environment as an otherworldly paradise.

THE DESIGN

All of the ryokan's 20 rooms are infused with a blend of east-meets-west, and all have views of the stunning gorge. The light-colored rooms feature **washi** sliding doors, **tatami** floors, and western beds. Six of the rooms are more luxurious suites that come with in-room baths, furnished wooden decks and floor-to-ceiling windows.

THE WATER

Hotel Iya Onsen is a member of the Japan Association of Secluded Hot Spring Inns, and many onsen pilgrims would travel all the way to this ryokan just for the exclusive **rotenburo** bathing experience located at the bottom of the valley.

In Hotel Iya Onsen's early years, the journey up and down the slope to the onsen was not the most convenient, to say the least. In 1984, a cable car was built to provide a more efficient route down to the valley. The self-operated cable car transports guests to the **rotenburo** by the river, descending down the 42-degree slope at a gradual pace. The panoramic view of the gorge is on full display during the five-minute ride.

There are gender-separated changing rooms at the bottom of the valley, attached to the two open-air Keikoku no Yu (渓谷の湯) and Seseragi no Yu (せせらぎの湯) hot spring baths built right beside the river. These baths would alternate between male and female use at a specific time each day. The spring water is piped from the source and continuously overflows from the onsen pools. The onsen water is opaque, due to its sulfur, sodium, calcium and potassium content. It is also slippery and bubbly due to its high alkaline bicarbonate properties — the entire surface is covered in bubbles and the soap-like water helps to soften the skin surface and gently wash away dead skin.

The water is maintained at the same temperature as the spring source, at around 38.3 degrees Celsius, and no plain water or chemicals are added to the mix. This lower-than-usual temperature allows guests to soak for a longer period of time.

There are communal indoor baths at the main building of Hotel Iya Onsen, where shower facilities are available and where guests can go when the rotenburo baths are closed.

THE CUISINE

Dinner at Hotel Iya Onsen is a succession of **kaiseki** courses served in the restaurant Café Dining Hana, which boasts splendid views of the gorge through wide glass windows. Head chef Yoshitaka Yamashita decides on the menu according to the seasons. The menu includes Iya mountain dishes consumed by locals, such as buckwheat grain soup; handmade soba noodles kneaded from 100 percent buckwheat (resulting in a much coarser texture and stronger flavors); small and dense Genpei Imo potatoes organically grown by local farmers in the terraced valley; as well as konjac, a rubbery gray gelatin made from Japanese yams. Freshly caught red-spotted river trout are served as sashimi, and Sudachi Ayu river fish from the nearby Yoshino River are char-grilled and presented in a bamboo basket. The main dishes are meats sourced from Tokushima — choose from Awa wagyu beef teppanyaki or Awa Kintoki pork omiki **nabe** (a hotpot using Japanese sake and miso soy sauce as soup base).

THE TAKEAWAY

Iya is at its most captivating on an autumn day, covered in low-hanging fog and with its mountains draped in fiery red and yellow.

Iya's mysterious, mesmerizing charm is fitting for a place that's shrouded in myths, folklore and foggy mountains. Hotel Iya Onsen has the best views of the gorge, and it's most exciting to ride the cable car down the steep valley for a soak in the bubbly onsen right next to the rushing river. I cherish those extraordinary moments I had sitting in the middle of the rocky gorge, pampered by the amazing scenery.

Wanoyado Hotel Iya Onsen
和の宿
ホテル祖谷温泉

Address
367-28 Ikeda, Matsuo, Matsumoto, Miyoshi, Tokushima Prefecture, 778-0165 | +81 883-75-2311

Website
www.iyaonsen.co.jp

Getting Here
Remote. By car: Drive from Osaka Kansai Airport (4hrs). By train: From the Osaka Kansai Airport, take the JR Limited Express train to Shin-Osaka Station (50min). Then hop on the Tokaido-Sanyo Shinkansen to Okayama Station (50min). Take the JR Dosan Line train to Oboke Station, where Hotel Iya Onsen offers free shuttle bus transfers (reserve in advance).

Price Range / Rooms
Mid-range. Traditional Japanese style.

ONSEN WATER

Type: A combination of Simple and Sulfur Springs

Color and Odor: Opaque; slightly sulfurous

pH: 9.1

Gensen Kakenagashi: Yes

Filtered and Circulated: No

Temperature at Source: 38.3°C

Temperature at Bath: 38.3°C

Mikiya, Hyogo Prefecture

三木屋　城崎温泉

THE STORY

The hot spring village of Kinosaki has been a centuries-old favorite for the Japanese, and is easily accessible from the cities of Osaka and Kyoto. This famous onsen town traces back to the Nara era — legend has it that Kinosaki Onsen was discovered around 717 CE when monk Douchi Shonin prayed for 1,000 days, prompting geothermal water to burst forth from the ground.

Kinosaki's traditions have been well-kept by the locals, and visitors today still have the luxury of immersing themselves in the timeless beauty of the old town by strolling along the picturesque canal and hopping to the seven famous public bathhouses in their colorful **yukata** garments and traditional Japanese wooden **geta** sandals.

Mikiya, a 300-year-old family-run traditional Japanese ryokan, was first established by the descendents of the Miki Castle soldiers who settled in Kinosaki. This historic ryokan has received many literary masters and painters through the ages, including Japanese novelist Naoya Shiga (also known as the "God of Novels"), where he wrote the famous short story "At Kinosaki" during his three-week stay in 1913. Room number 26 is his most favorite room of all.

Daisuke Kataoka is the 10th-generation owner of Mikiya, and he works together with his wife Risa Kataoka, who is the **okami** of the ryokan. Mr. Kataoka has been managing Mikiya for 10 years, and his most memorable moment was when an old couple who celebrated their honeymoon 50 years ago at Mikiya revisited the ryokan for their golden anniversary. Mrs. Kataoka personally greets arriving guests every day, and can communicate fluently in English.

THE DESIGN

Mikiya consists of an elegant three-story wooden building that was rebuilt in 1927 after the original building was destroyed by the Tajima Earthquake in 1925. Parts of the interior, like the lobby and the restaurant, have been modernized. The rest of the space has kept its original antique glamor, featuring well-preserved dark-brown wooden pillars, beams, corridors, and creaky wooden floors.

The rooms feature classic ryokan elements of **washi** screen doors, **tatami**-matted floors, low wooden tables, and views of an elegant traditional Japanese courtyard. In 2014, Mikiya's building was designated a Registered Tangible Cultural Property by the Japanese government to protect its historical and artistic values.

THE WATER

The onsen town of Kinosaki boasts a 1,400-year history, attracting onsen lovers who come for the seven public onsen baths dispersed throughout the town. Each public onsen has its own unique style, design, and atmosphere, using spring water from various sources in the village. Guests staying overnight at any of the ryokan lodges in Kinosaki would usually receive a pass from the ryokan that would give them free access to all seven bathhouses. Kinosaki is one of the few onsen towns in Japan that allow visitors with tattoos in without any questions.

At Mikiya, hot spring water is piped into two gender-separated indoor baths from a tank located in the town's main Onsen Street, with water extracted from the same spring sources as Kinosaki village and distributed to various accommodations in Kinosaki. It is said to soothe cuts and burns, as well as to alleviate muscular pain. Most people visiting Kinosaki would prefer the fun of soaking at the public bathhouses, and so the onsen baths at Mikiya are usually a more private, tranquil experience.

THE CUISINE

Kinosaki is located near the Sea of Japan in the old province of Tajima (birthplace of Kobe beef), blessed by an abundant supply of high-quality ingredients. Dinner at Mikiya is an extravagant **kaiseki** affair, served at the modern Japanese-style Heihachiro dining hall.

The head chef would decide on the seasonal menu along with the ryokan owner, sourcing the freshest from the region's farms. The meal may include squid, sea bream and amberjack sashimi; local vegetables like sweet potato and baked eggplant; and char-grilled Tajima wagyu, highly prized for its beautifully minced marbled meat.

During the winter months, the menu would include the region's quintessential Matsuba crab, likely to be the finest crab in Japan and only available seasonally. This premium snow crab is caught from the port of Tsuiyama, and carries a blue tag to prove its origin — harvesting is strictly restricted to between November to March. At Mikiya, guests can savor Matsuba crab's soft and succulent meat cooked various ways. For instance, it might be grilled over charcoal fire and lightly seasoned with sea salt and dipped into an intensely flavored kani miso (crab tomalley); or boiled in a **shabu shabu** hotpot broth that makes the crabmeat fluffy and open up like a flower.

ONSEN WATER

Type: Chloride Spring (with sodium, calcium elements)

Color and Odor: Colorless; odorless

pH: 9.1

Gensen Kakenagashi: No

Filtered and Circulated: Yes

Temperature at Source: 42°C to 45°C

Temperature at Bath: 42°C

THE TAKEAWAY

There is much charm in the picturesque old town of Kinosaki: the low-hanging weeping willows and clusters of pink cherry blossoms lined along the canals fill the air with romance. Traditional sukiya houses (villa-like buildings with tea house aesthetics) are turned into shops that sell local crafts and snacks, and visitors would drop by while making their way to the public bathhouses. I had fun clip-clopping through the bustling streets in **geta** sandals and a floral-patterned **yukata**, carrying a straw-knitted bathing basket around.

Mikiya's wooden architecture makes for a gorgeous building. I was assigned to beautiful room number 20, with a sliding glass door that opens to a harmony-filled Japanese garden. I was captivated by the dark-wood charm of the building, and impressed by how well it has been preserved. I felt fortunate to be here, to be able to honor the centuries-long traditions that Mikiya's ancestors have safeguarded and passed on.

Mikiya
三木屋

Address
487 Kinosaki, Yushima, Toyooka, Hyogo Prefecture, 669-6101 | +81 796-32-2031

Website
www.kinosaki-mikiya.jp

Getting Here
Convenient. From Osaka station, take the JR Kounotori Limited Express Line to Kinosaki Onsen Station (2.5 hrs); From Kyoto station, take the JR Kinosaki Limited Express to Kinosaki Onsen Station (2.5 hrs).

Price Range / Rooms
Mid-range. Traditional Japanese style.

Suisen, Kyoto Prefecture

湯の花温泉

翠泉

Photo: Suisen

THE STORY

Tucked away in the natural surrounds of Yunohana Onsen town in Kyoto Prefecture, Suisen is a traditional Japanese ryokan that offers a quiet retreat, in contrast to bustling, touristy Kyoto. There are plenty of sightseeing spots near Suisen, including Sagano's bamboo forest; Tenryuji Temple; the Togetsukyo bridge; and the stunning Hozukyo Valley between Arashiyama and Kameoka, viewable from a ride on the Sagano Scenic Railway and famous for its autumn foliage.

Suisen first opened in the 1860s and was originally a Samurai-hosting venue in central Kyoto. It relocated to its current location more than 30 years ago. Nowadays, Suisen welcomes guests aged six or above and groups of not more than 10 to ensure an intimate experience for all.

THE DESIGN

Guests are pampered and exposed to authentic Kyoto culture and heritage at Suisen. The traditional decor and artwork found inside give the ryokan a subtle elegance. Upon arrival, guests will be seated at the lobby lounge, which faces an enchanting traditional Japanese Zen garden filled with cherry blossom, maple, and bonsai trees and raked gravel paths that mimic water ripples. Traditional matcha (powdered green tea) and sweets are served upon arrival.

The 13 rooms are all generous in space and refurbished with contemporary touches while retaining traditional Japanese aesthetics. The warm and cozy ambience puts the mind at peace. Rooms are furnished with western-style beds placed on top of a **tatami**-matted floor; seven of the rooms feature a private outdoor bath. The biggest and most luxurious of them all is the 113-square meter Suisen Suite, featuring a half-sheltered hinoki (Japanese cypress) onsen bath that sits on a wide balcony with luscious views of the surrounding greenery.

Photo: Suisen

THE WATER

Legend has it that warriors during the Sengoku period (circa 1467 to 1600) would go to Yunohana after a day of battle to heal their injuries in the restorative hot spring. The warm, rare-to-find radium spring water is piped into two gender-separated communal baths as well as the in-room private baths, heated to about 42 degrees Celsius. The water is colorless and odorless and contains safe, trace amounts of radiation believed to be highly therapeutic for neuropathic and muscular pain, chronic digestive illnesses, as well as fatigue. Each communal bath has an outdoor and indoor onsen pool that is either stone- or cypress-lined, overlooking the Japanese garden. You will find a kusari-doi ("rain chain") hung next to the bath: it is extremely calming to watch rainwater dripping through a series of metal cups and listen to the trickling sounds produced by such a device.

ONSEN WATER

Type: Radium Spring

Color and Odor: Colorless; odorless

pH: 8.4

Gensen Kakenagashi: No

Filtered and Circulated: Yes

Temperature at Source: 29.2°C

Temperature at Bath: 42°C

THE CUISINE

In keeping with Kyoto's traditions, dining at Suisen is a fancy **kaiseki** affair. Expect a procession of gourmet delicacies boasting the best of local produce. Behind the scenes is head chef Hideo Yamamori, who joined Suisen in 2018. Yamamori pays attention to every detail, from meeting with local farmers for ingredients, to designing the seasonal menu and preparing the exquisite dishes with his team. Dinner is served in private dining rooms. Food-wise, think Kyoto-grown eggplant in sesame dressing served in delicate glassware; pumpkin and lotus root dumplings in clear fish broth; and lightly seared tuna and sashimi of the day. Other outstanding dishes include a grilled ayu fish; a Tamba beef **shabu shabu**; eight kinds of grilled seafood and seasonal vegetables, as well as a fragrant steamed rice with scallop, shimeji mushroom and burdock.

Breakfast is also an elaborate treat featuring a selection of pickled vegetables, yogurt, and salad neatly placed in a nine-compartment bento, grilled premium fish nodoguro (blackthroat seaperch), and Kyoto's famous **yuba** (layered tofu skin).

Suisen
翠泉

Address
6-3 Inoshiri, Ashinoyama, Hiedano,
Kameoka, Kyoto Prefecture,
621-0034 | +81 771-22-7575

Website
www.kyoto-suisen.com

Getting Here
Convenient. From Kyoto station, take
the JR Sagano Line to Kameoka Station
(20min), then transfer to the ryokan's
free shuttle bus to Suisen (15min).
Shuttle must be reserved in advance.

Rooms
High-end. Traditional
Japanese style.

THE TAKEAWAY

It was a hot and rainy August day when
I visited Suisen after a long journey. I was
much relieved upon my arrival, settling
in with some welcome tea and sweets
while looking out towards the elegant
Japanese courtyard. Suisen is a beautiful
ryokan. It was an indulgence to be able
to pamper myself in traditional Kyoto-
style fashion.

During dinner, I had the pleasure to meet
with chef Yamamori. He came to present
the grilled ayu fish, which was freshly
caught, charcoal-grilled and served on a
plate coated with black paint. He created
a hand-drawn waterfall and moon on the
plate by spreading powdered salt using a
feather pen. It was so vivid, it was as if the
ayu fish were swimming on the plate. I was
completely in awe of this masterpiece.

Beniya Mukayu, Ishikawa Prefecture

山代温泉 べにや無何有

THE STORY

Beniya Mukayu is an award-winning ryokan with a luxuriously Zen atmosphere, where Japanese sensibilities and western elements harmoniously meet. It is located in the renowned Yamashiro Onsen town of Kaga, Ishikawa Prefecture.

The word mukayu means "non-existence", a term that originally came from Chinese philosopher Zhuangzi in 4th century BC. His philosophy of "richness in emptiness" is well integrated into Beniya Mukayu's ethos. The Zen-based minimalist interior is sparsely decorated, with earthy elements, allowing guests to experience philosophical emptiness and freedom during their stay. The owners have much appreciation for Ishikawa's long history of arts and culture: fine Japanese ceramics and lacquerware are displayed throughout the space, adding much elegance

to the ryokan. Beniya Mukayu has been a member of the Relais & Chateaux since 2008, and has received many awards throughout the years.

The success of Beniya Mukayu is thanks to more than 90 years of hard work by the Nakamichi family. Kazunari Nakamichi and his wife Sachiko Nakamichi are the current third-generation proprietors. It all began when Mr. Nakamichi's grandfather started a noodle shop near Yamashiro Onsen Street and later transformed it into a small 10-room Japanese inn in 1928. In 1970, Mr. Nakamichi's father relocated the ryokan to its present address on the Yamashiro hillside and expanded it to 46 rooms.

THE DESIGN

The owners decided to rebuild the ryokan in 1993, and the building that we see now was rebuilt and redesigned in phases by renowned architect Kiyoshi Sey Takayama. Both Mr. and Mrs. Nakamichi are very involved in the ongoing upgrades of the hotel. The most recent project included the Byakuroku Suite, completed in 2018: the Byakuroku comes with a secluded garden bath and a quiet study corner designed to help invigorate one's creative juices and energy levels.

There are now 17 rooms at Beniya Mukayu, and all feature contemporary Zen designs like bamboo flooring and a wide balcony that overlooks the maple and cherry blossom Japanese garden.

THE WATER

According to legend, Yamashiro Onsen was discovered in the Jinki period (725 CE) by monk Gyoki, who saw a crow healing its wounds using Yamashiro's hot spring water. Yamashiro Onsen was also frequently used by samurais and generals to restore health.

The gender-separated Komorebi no Yu (こもれびの湯) communal baths have indoor and outdoor half open-air pools that draw pure hot spring water from two underground sources. Guests can also enjoy their own private indoor or outdoor bath in the rooms.

The water varies from 40 to 44 degrees Celsius due to seasonal fluctuations. Rich in calcium and sodium, the water is said to aid with health conditions such as hypertension, arteriosclerosis and rheumatism. Thanks to the high level of sodium present, the water helps to smooth the skin by removing dead skin cells and impurities from one's body.

THE CUISINE

Dining at Beniya Mukayu is an exquisite experience that highlights the best of Kaga's culinary traditions. The owners and chef meet regularly to refresh the menu according to the seasonal ingredients available.

Meals are served at the restaurant Kaiseki Horin. Dinner is an exciting journey of traditional Japanese **kaiseki** dishes prepared with a modern twist, with ingredients sourced from organic farmers and top producers in the region.

You will learn about the making of each dish from the detailed explanations of the friendly staff. Ishikawa Prefecture is blessed with superior seafood choices from the Sea of Japan, like the snow crabs that are only available from November to March each year.

Guests are presented with a menu of the night, handwritten and hand-drawn by Mrs. Nakamichi. Some outstanding dishes include a clam, shrimp, and lotus root broth served in a mini winter melon; seasonal assorted vegetables; and a char-grilled rockfish wrapped in bamboo leaves. A fine wine or sake selected by the owners to go with the meal is highly recommended.

Guests have the option of either a Japanese- or western-style breakfast. Coffee lovers need to give Mukayu's original house blend a go.

ONSEN WATER

Type: Sulfate Spring
(with sodium, calcium elements)

Color and Odor: Colorless; odorless

pH: 8.3

Gensen Kakenagashi: Yes

Filtered and Circulated: No

Temperature at Source: 46.4°C

Temperature at Bath: 40°C to 44°C

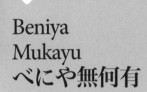

Beniya
Mukayu
べにや無何有

Address
55-1-3 Yamashiro Onsen, Kaga,
Ishikawa Prefecture, 922-0242 |
+81 761-77-1340

Website
mukayu.com

Getting Here
Convenient. Take the
Hokuriku Shinkansen Line
from Tokyo Station to Kaga
Onsen Station (3hrs). Beniya
Mukayu can arrange free
shuttle bus pick-up from the
Kaga Onsen train station.

Rooms
High-end. Contemporary
Japanese and western style.

THE TAKEAWAY

Beniya Mukayu is an indulgent retreat for
the body and mind. My mind feels emptied
after a relaxing night of onsen cleansing.
Mr. and Mrs. Nakamichi would personally
send off guests every morning, dressed
elegantly in their traditional kimonos. The
admirable couple have earned many loyal
customers over the years through their
hard work and forward-thinking business
vision. I respect their desire to promote
traditional ryokan heritage and Japanese
hospitality to the world.

While staying at Beniya Mukayu, guests
get to attend a traditional Japanese
tea ceremony at the Eiraku-An Tea
Ceremony Room, where Mr. Nakamichi
would prepare and serve some matcha.
Meanwhile, Mrs. Nakamichi holds free
yoga classes every morning.

白骨温泉

湯元齋藤旅館

THE STORY

Yumoto Saito is the largest and oldest of 10 ryokan accommodations at Shirahone Onsen in Nagano Prefecture. Nestled deep in the hot spring town at an altitude of 1,400 meters in the Japanese Alps, the ryokan is surrounded by tranquil mountains and forests — the enchanting scenery is a source of inspiration for poets and writers alike.

Before the Taisho era (1912-1926), Shirahone was called Shirafune (白舟 , "white ship") because the thick white layer of mineral deposits found in an onsen tub here was said to resemble a big white ship. But when writer Nakazato Kaizan's novel "Great Bodhisattva Pass" later referred to it as Shirahone (白骨 , "white bone"), everyone else followed suit.

The family-run Yumoto Saito was established in 1738, and is currently managed by seventh generation owner Muranaka Sosuke. The ryokan covers a large swath of land that has expanded over time and now consists of several renovated historical buildings.

THE DESIGN

The guest rooms in each annex at Yumoto Saito are of different designs, and some overlook the gorgeous valley or river down the gorge. The Showakan（昭和館）, Kaizansou（介山荘）and Bokusuisou（牧水荘）buildings feature elegant and traditional Japanese-style rooms with **tatami**-matted floors, **washi** paper sliding doors, and futons and western-style beds. The Bokusui-sou and Kaizan-sou were named after Japanese poet Bokusui Wakayama and writer Nakazato Kaizan, who have both stayed at Yumoto Saito. The Kaizan-sou boasts some of the most luxurious suites in the ryokan — it is also furthest away from the main building. The special suites here come with a semi-open-air onsen, floor-to-ceiling windows, and a wooden deck on which to enjoy the enchanting forest views.

THE WATER

The milky water found here is legendary. There's an ancient saying at Shirahone Onsen that if you bathe here for three days, you won't catch a cold for three years. Shirahone's spring is commonly referred to as a reisen（霊泉 , "miraculous spring"）by the locals, due to its alleged highly therapeutic effects. Warriors and mine workers as far back as the Kamakura period (1185–1333) were said to come to Shirahone Onsen to treat their injuries and illnesses.

There are more than 10 hot spring sources at Shirahone. Yumoto Saito sources its water from four artesian springs that naturally gush at about 116 liters per hour. The bubbly

bicarbonate sulfur-based water contains sulfur, calcium and carbon dioxide, and is completely transparent when it first bursts through the ground. The sulfur particles in the water then crystallize when exposed to the air, subsequently turning the water a milky white. The color and temperature of the water varies depending on the season. Shirahone's sulfuric water has an almost-neutral acidity of pH6.7, which is a rare find. This makes the water extra gentle on the skin.

There are two gender-separated communal bathhouses at Yumoto Saito: the Ryujin no Yu (龍神の湯) and the Yakushi no Yu (薬師の湯). You will find indoor and semi-open-air onsen pools in both. The mineral deposits from the water harden and accumulate over time, coating the pools' wooden frames in white.

Meanwhile, the Oniga-jo (鬼が城) is a large **rotenburo** that allows guests to be much closer to nature. Soaking in this outdoor bath in the middle of the forest is pure bliss. The water is maintained at a body-friendly temperature of around 39 degrees Celsius.

The water is said to be especially helpful for digestive illnesses, and can actually be consumed via designated water taps provided by most of the ryokan lodgings in the area.

ONSEN WATER

Type: A combination of Bicarbonate and Sulfur Springs (with magnesium, calcium elements)

Color and Odor: Opaque milky white; slightly sulfurous

pH: 6.7

Gensen Kakenagashi: Yes

Filtered and Circulated: No

Temperature at Source: 35°C to 45°C

Temperature at Bath: 39°C

THE CUISINE

Yumoto Saito serves a simple multi-course **kaiseki** meal at the restaurant in the Showa-kan building. The menu changes monthly, but some of the signature dishes are available all year round, like the grilled Shinshu wagyu beef; the Shinshu-bred premium beef sukiyaki; and the made-to-order slow-grilled rockfish. There might be a freshly made tofu dish or two. At the end of the meal, enjoy a hearty rice porridge cooked in Shirahone onsen water, paired with pickled Nozawa vegetables.

THE TAKEAWAY

I had the pleasure of meeting with owner Muranaka Sosuke during my stay. Born and raised in Shirahone, he continues to build on his family's legacy. It was early December when I visited Yumoto Saito. Heavy snowfall overnight turned Shirahone into a winter wonderland. It was such a pretty scene from my balcony, with the stillness of winter in full view. The serene mountains of Shirahone were dusted in snow — I totally understand why this place is such an inspiration for creative people.

Yumoto Saito
湯元齋藤旅館

Address
4195 Shirahone Onsen, Azumi, Matsumoto, Nagano Prefecture, 390-1515 | +81 263-93-2311

Website
www.shirahone.net

Getting Here
Remote. By Train: From Tokyo Station, take the JR Azusa Limited Express train to Matsumoto station (3hrs), then take the Matsumoto Dentetsu to get to Shin-Shimashima station, and take a bus run by the Alpico Bus Company to reach Shirahone Onsen station. Yumoto Saito offers free shuttle bus pickup from the Shirahone Onsen bus station. By Car: Drive from Tokyo to Shirahone Onsen (4hrs).

Price Range / Rooms
Mid-range. Traditional Japanese style.

Satoyama Jujo, Niigata Prefecture

大沢山温泉

里山十帖

THE STORY

Satoyama Jujo is located in the mountainous, northern part of Niigata Prefecture in the Minami-Uonuma region, where the country's highest quality Koshihikari rice is grown on beautiful terraced rice paddies.

When founder and creative director Toru Iwasa opened Satoyama Jujo in 2014, he thought of an innovative way to redefine luxury. Knowing that travelers are hungry for inspirational experiences nowadays, Iwasa created a ryokan that creatively communicates 10 different aspects of Satoyama Jujo, from its dining offerings to its architecture.

Born and raised in Tokyo, Iwasa is the president and editor-in-chief of the popular Jiyujin lifestyle magazine that he started in 2000. He moved to Minami-Uonuma in 2004 to cultivate rice, hoping to seek a slower, simpler and better quality of life in the natural mountainous landscapes of Niigata. Satoyama Jujo is a continuation of his many projects.

With an occupancy rate of over 90 percent within 3 months of opening, it has almost always been fully booked since, and reservations need to be made months in advance.

THE DESIGN

The one-of-a-kind experience at Satoyama Jujo begins when you slip off your shoes at the Reception Hall. Walk into a 150-year-old timber structure made entirely from keyaki hardwood, constructed to withstand the weight of heavy snowfall in this region. The interior has been meticulously restored. Satoyama Jujo's old-world charms, like the stunning lacquer-coated wooden beams and floors, are a nice contrast to the modern designer furniture and contemporary Japanese artwork displayed inside. The most remarkable piece is the "Lucky Hammer" sculpted entirely from an enormous camphor tree trunk by award-winning artist Ryuichi Ohira, exhibited at the Reception Hall.

The annex is a new building that extends from the old house and features 13 modern guest rooms, all with views overlooking the forest or the mountains. No two rooms have the same design, but all feature Japanese and contemporary elements.

THE WATER

The outdoor hot spring bath Amanogawa (天の川) at Satoyama Jujo offers some magnificent views of Mount Makihata. The area has been carefully landscaped to ensure that no man-made structure would obstruct the scenery while one soaks in the infinity pool-inspired bath.

The scene is distinctly gorgeous during winter, when the faraway mountain ranges are coated in white snow. Two gender-separated **rotenburo** baths of different designs are available, and they alternate between female and male guest use each morning. The silky smooth alkaline water here is high in sodium, potassium and calcium. At a rather low temperature of 27 degrees Celsius at the source, the water is heated to 40 to 43 degrees Celsius for the onsen baths.

THE CUISINE

Satoyama Jujo's restaurant Sanaburi serves simple and distinctive dishes that mainly consist of vegetables and rice. A carefully curated western wine and Japanese sake list is available to pair with the dishes.

Food director Yutaka Kitazaki was trained in a three-star Michelin traditional Japanese restaurant in Kyoto and had his own restaurant in Kanazawa before joining Satoyama Jujo. The ryokan's unique concept provides the perfect environment for him to create artistic dishes using ingredients like wild mountain vegetables that are only seasonally available at Minami-Uonuma.

Spring would see wild ferns and shoots at the table; while locally grown seasonal vegetables, seafood from the Sea of Japan, wagyu beef, and Echigo pork would be available the rest of the year. Vegetables are also pickled in preparation for snowy winters. Kitazaki redefines luxury cuisine by making delicious dishes from humble ingredients.

One must try the Niigata Koshihikari rice while at Satoyama Jujo; it is of the most superior rice grade in Japan. Guests can steam their own Koshihikari rice right at their table, using a beautiful double-lid earthenware pot to preserve its nutrients and taste. The entire process takes about 30 minutes, and the end product is exceptionally delicious, with the perfect firmness, consistency and sweetness.

THE TAKEAWAY

Satoyama Jujo is truly a unique modern ryokan that offers an array of interesting activities for guests. During my winter visit, I was completely captivated by the views of the snow-capped mountain ranges along the border of Gunma and Niigata Prefectures, both from my room and from the Amanogawa **rotenburo**. I had the most fun cooking my own pot of Koshihikari rice at the dining table. So delicious it was! The experience also reminded me of my Asian roots, and how important rice cultivation has been in Asian culture.

Satoyama Jujo
里山十帖

Address
1209-6 Osawa, Minamiuonuma, Niigata
Prefecture, 949-6361 | +81 25-783-6777

Website
en.satoyama-jujo.com

Getting Here
Convenient. From Tokyo, take the
Joetsu Shinkansen in Tokyo Station to
Osawa Station (80min), then transfer
to Satoyama Jujo's free shuttle bus
available at designated times of the day.

Price Range / Rooms
High-end. Contemporary Japanese
and Western style.

ONSEN
WATER

Type: A combination of Chloride
and Carbonated Springs
(with sodium elements)

Color and Odor: Colorless; odorless

pH: 8.46

Gensen Kakenagashi: No

Filtered and Circulated: Yes

Temperature at Source: 27.2°C

Temperature at Bath: 40°C to 43°C

Naraya, Gunma Prefecture

奈良屋　草津温泉

THE STORY

Naraya is a family-run ryokan founded by a man named Toyokichi Kobayashi in 1877; it is regarded as one of the most reputable traditional Japanese ryokan offerings in the onsen town of Kusatsu. Yoshinobu Kobayashi is the current sixth-generation owner.

Kusatsu itself is situated in the Northwestern part of Gunma Prefecture, at an altitude of 1,200 meters, near the active volcano Mount Kusatsu-Shirane. Most famous for being home to Japan's largest volume of highly therapeutic, acidic thermal waters, Kusatsu has no trouble attracting local and international visitors alike each year.

Kusatsu's ancestors have adopted a method of naturally lowering the temperature of the original hot spring water by rhythmically beating the water with a long wooden plank, without adding any plain cold water to the mix. This method, also known as yumomi (湯もみ), has been in practice since the Edo period. Yumomi dances are still performed today: a group of local women in traditional garb and towel-wrapped hair would sing and dance while celebrating this ancient tradition.

Photo: Naraya

THE DESIGN

Naraya is situated in the middle of Kusatsu, at an ideal location right next to the Yubatake (湯畑) hot spring, the town's main attraction. Following strict town rules, Naraya's building architecture is very well preserved, keeping its original exterior wooden facade intact.

There are 36 guest rooms in Naraya, ranging from standard **tatami**-matted spaces with comfortable futons to more luxurious rooms with western-style beds. Some rooms come with views of the Yubatake hot spring.

THE WATER

Legend has it that Kusatsu's hot springs were discovered more than 1,800 years ago. The region is renowned for its large volume of free-flowing, therapeutic and highly acidic hot springs with a low pH of 2.0, gushing out at roughly 65 degrees Celsius. The amount of water flowing from the sources is a hard-to-believe 32,000 liters per minute — the highest in Japan. As a result, the strong smell of sulfur fills the air here.

During the Edo and Meiji periods, Kusatsu was so popular that the baths became congested with samurais, shoguns, and the general public trying to rehabilitate from their different ailments. Dr. Erwin Von Bälz, a German who was appointed court physician to emperor Meiji in 1902 (aka the father of western medicine in Japan), studied Kusatsu's waters extensively.

Naraya's waters come from Kusatsu's oldest water source, the Shirahata Gensen (白旗源泉). It is brought to the ryokan by gravity; amazingly, no extraction or piping is necessary. The water is collected in wooden troughs and gradually cooled overnight before being gently flowed into the baths.

At Naraya, the longstanding tradition of employing a yumori — an onsen master — is alive and well. The yumori is in charge of monitoring the water and maintaining the most suitable bath temperatures (roughly 42 degrees Celsius).

There are indoor and outdoor pools for each of the gender-separated communal baths at the ryokan's lowest level. The water contains sulfur and aluminum, which are said to be highly effective against bacteria and fungus growth, as well as in relieving muscular pain and more. The hydrogen sulfide in the water crystallizes into **yunohana** (湯の花 , an insoluble deposit that floats in the water) when exposed to air and sunlight. **Yunohana** forms a membrane over one's skin, making it feel particularly soft. Bathers frequently immerse themselves into the milky water, close their eyes, and say a prayer — not only to seek relaxation but also in hopes of healing their bodies.

Meanwhile, a visit to the nearby Sainokawara Rotenburo (西の河 原露天風呂) is a must. For a small fee, you can take refuge in the huge 500-square-meter thermal pool.

THE CUISINE

Dinner and breakfast are served in the restaurant's elegant private rooms, featuring seasonal local specialties of mountain vegetables and produce, from rainbow trout to fragrant matsutake mushrooms. The staff welcomes guests with a serving of local sake before presenting an elegantly arranged **kaiseki** dinner. The executive chef changes the menu every one to two months, according to the season. The Japanese-style breakfast is nutritious and well-balanced, featuring grilled cod, vegetable stews, onsen tamago (eggs half-cooked in hot onsen water), miso soup and a variety of lightly seasoned pickles.

THE TAKEAWAY

Naraya takes pride in heritage preservation. I had the honor of meeting with Naraya's yumori, Takao Nakazawa, during my stay. Nakazawa is Naraya's sixth-generation yumori. He acquired the techniques to manage the onsen water from the previous master. Much respect to him, he who has dedicated more than 20 years to this unique profession.

ONSEN WATER

Type: A combination of Sulfate and Chloride Springs (with sulfur, aluminum elements)

Color and Odor: Slightly cloudy white; slightly sulfurous

pH: 2.0

Gensen Kakenagashi: Yes

Filtered and Circulated: No

Temperature at Source: 65°C

Temperature at Bath: 43°C

Naraya
奈良屋

Address
396 Kusatsu, Agatsuma,
Gunma Prefecture, 377-1711 |
+81 279-88-2311

Website
www.kusatsu-naraya.co.jp

Getting Here
Remote. Take Shinkansen
from Tokyo Station to Takasaki
Station (3hrs), then transfer
to Nagano Hara Kusatsuguchi
Station by train. Take a bus
bound for Kusatsuto Kusatsu
Bus Terminal. Walk from
Kusatsu Bus Terminal to
Naraya (3min).

Price Range / Rooms
Mid-range. Traditional
Japanese style.

Hoshi Onsen Chojukan, Gunma Prefecture

長寿館

法師温泉

THE STORY

A charming and historic ryokan tucked in the Joshinetsu-Kogen National Park in the town of Minakami in Gunma Prefecture, Hoshi Onsen Chojukan is highly regarded for its quality onsen water and warm hospitality. As a member of the Japan Association of Secluded Hot Spring Inns, the ryokan attracts numerous onsen pilgrims every year.

It takes a 20-minute drive through a long narrow road to reach Hoshi Onsen Chojukan, which sits deep inside the National Park. Upon arrival, the ryokan's old-Japan vibes will bring you back in time. You will find old posters, photographs and art pieces on the walls along the corridors.

Hoshi Onsen Chojukan was named after the Japanese Buddhist monk Kobo Daishi, who was believed to have discovered the source of the onsen water more than 1,300 years ago. This ryokan was established in 1875 by the Okamura family and continues to be family-owned.

Takeshi Okamura, the seventh-generation proprietor, has taken the helm at Hoshi and runs the ryokan along with his father. He takes pride in his family heritage and hopes to keep passing the baton to future generations. His long-serving crew goes above and beyond to ensure that guests enjoy their stay.

THE DESIGN

The architecture at Hoshi is remarkable. The elegant and rustic Meiji period-style building is built entirely from cypress and chestnut trees found in the surrounding forest.

The two-story ryokan consists of four wings: the Honkan main building; the Bekkan (別館 , annex); and the more recently built Kunzanso (薫山荘) and Horyuden (法隆殿) annexes. The Honkan and Bekkan buildings have both been recognized as National Registered Tangible Cultural Properties by the Japanese government. It is impressive that the century-old buildings show no signs of wear and tear. There are 33 rooms in Hoshi, and 32 of them are traditional Japanese style with **tatami** flooring. The remaining room is a combination of Japanese and western styles. All rooms are equipped with a **kotatsu**.

One of the most charming rooms is Room 31 in the Kunsanzo annex, built next to the Hoshi River and featuring four calligraphy scrolls that are adhered to the sliding doors. During the summer, the balcony outside offers a gentle symphony of birdsong and the sounds of the river. Meanwhile, the special Yashio no Ma suite in the Horyuden annex comes with a fireplace and western-style beds.

Photo: Hoshi Onsen

Photo: Hoshi Onsen

THE WATER

The quality of the water at Hoshi has been a well-kept secret for more than 100 years. The Okamura family believes it is important to understand the ecosystem and environment surrounding Hoshi in order to maintain the water's quality. The family has ensured that the hot spring water composition at Hoshi is the same as it has always been. Hoshi's hot spring is a rare-to-find **jifunsen** (自噴泉 , "artesian spring"), with 433 liters of water naturally gushing out of the ground every minute. The water contains calcium and sodium sulfates, which are said to help with gastrointestinal disorders, burns, and other ailments as well as to soothe and moisturize the skin.

Hoshi no Yu (法師乃湯) is the main communal bath at Hoshi — it's a **konyoku** (mixed-gender bath) built right above the spring source. This antique wooden structure is surrounded by atypical arch-shaped windows, adding to the sacred atmosphere. The large cypress-lined bathtub is subdivided and filled with clear and soothing 41-degree-Celsius alkaline water. Every evening, the 8pm to 10pm slot is reserved for women's exclusive use.

The other two baths at Hoshi are Tamaki no Yu (玉城乃湯) and Choju no Yu (長寿 乃湯). There are designated periods during the day for the different genders to enjoy these baths separately.

THE CUISINE

Dinner at Hoshi is a traditional Japanese **kaiseki** affair, served either in the restaurant or in the room. Ingredients consist of freshly picked mountain vegetables and meat from Gunma's local farms. Special items include the sukiyaki Akagi beef and grilled iwana fish, a freshwater river fish caught in the wild streams nearby.

Hoshi's selection of **nihonshu** is from some of Gunma's best breweries. Rice from Niigata prefecture, cooked in Hoshi River mountain spring water, is also served.

Photo: Hoshi Onsen

THE TAKEAWAY

Hoshi's bathhouse is truly a sanctuary. I was completely beguiled by the beauty of the charming wooden cathedral-like structure. It felt spectacular to soak in the cypress tub and feel the water seep through from underneath the pebble bed, bubbling to the top. This incredible ryokan experience made me feel tranquil and forget about time.

As a tradition, Okamura-san likes to invite his guests to sit by the **irori** for a chat. He spent almost three hours to share interesting stories of Hoshi with me. I have the deepest admiration and respect for the humble Okamura family and their century of hard work and dedication in preserving the ryokan.

Hoshi Onsen Chojukan
法師温泉 長寿館

Address
650 Nagai, Minakami,
Tone, Gunma Prefecture,
379-1401 | +81 278-66-0005

Website
hoshi-onsen.com

Getting Here
Convenient. From Tokyo Station,
take the Shinkansen Joetsu Line to
Jomo-Kogen Station (1hr15min),
then take the bus to Sarugakyo bus
station and transfer to the connecting
bus to Hoshi Onsen (50min). There are
four buses available per day.

Price Range / Rooms
Mid-range. Traditional Japanese style.

ONSEN WATER

Type: Hoshi no Yu, Choju no Yu:
Sulfate Spring (with sodium,
calcium elements) | Tamaki no Yu:
Simple Spring

Color and Odor: Colorless; odorless

pH: 8.5

Gensen Kakenagashi: Yes

Filtered and Circulated: No

Temperature at Source: 41.5°C

Temperature at Bath: 41.5°C

Tatsumikan, Gunma Prefecture

上牧温泉

辰巳館

THE STORY

Open since 1924, and once a favorite hangout for highly regarded artist Kiyoshi Yamashita, Tatsumikan is a traditional Japanese ryokan in the Minamaki Kamimoku Onsen area of Gunma Prefecture, located at the foot of Mount Tanigawa and easily accessible by Shinkansen from Tokyo.

Takuya Fukatsu is the fourth-generation proprietor of Tatsumikan. His grandmother took over the management of Tatsumikan from the original owner, who had no heir to carry on the ryokan business. He is running the ryokan with his wife Kayoko Fukatsu, the **okami** in charge of operations. The humble couple delivers heart-warming hospitality, and their kindness has earned many loyal customers over the years. Fukatsu runs his ryokan according to three "warmth" mottos: the warmth of the onsen soothes the body; the warmth of the staff relaxes the mind; and the warmth of the charcoal fire dinners satisfies the palate.

THE DESIGN

Tatsumikan is situated in a picture-perfect town with an abundance of quality water, mountains and farmland. The ryokan is traditionally styled and features **tatami** floors. Most of the rooms face the scenic Tone River and Mount Tanigawa. Tone River is the second-longest river in Japan, serving up to 70 percent of the water supply to Tokyo residents. The Minakami region was designated as a UNESCO Biosphere Reserve in 2017 due to its distinct biological diversity.

THE WATER

The picturesque Minakami region attracts many visitors each year who seek a quiet onsen retreat, including creative types like poets and artists. There are a number of onsen baths available at Tatsumikan, but the signature offering is the Haniwa (はにわ) indoor communal bath, where you will find a stunning mosaic on the wall inside the bath house. This wall mosaic is a replica of Japanese contemporary artist Kiyoshi Yamashita's masterpiece, "Omine Swamp and Mount Tanigawa" (大峰沼と谷川岳). Yamashita is commonly referred to as the "Japanese Van

Gogh", and his original work consists of a paper collage depicting the beautiful autumn foliage at Omine Lake and Mount Tanigawa.

The chloride sulfate spring with sodium elements at Tatsumikan is colorless, odorless, and potable. The water comes from the melted snow on Mount Tanigawa, stored underground and heated by the earth's geothermal energy before being extracted from the source and transported to the baths. The clear water is said to increase the skin's moisture and elasticity, and help to alleviate symptoms from rheumatism and even frozen shoulders and hemorrhoids.

Besides the Haniwa, there are five other onsen baths available to guests, including the large Tamayura no Yu (たまゆらの湯) **rotenburo** with Japanese garden view; the Kawasemi no Yu (かわせみの湯) indoor bath lined with fragrant cypress wood; the Hisui no Yu (ひすいの湯); and two private baths with jacuzzi and steam sauna attached.

THE CUISINE

Tatsumikan offers Irori Kansan-yaki, or a style of charcoal-grilled mountain village cuisine. The ryokan takes pride in sourcing domestic Gunma ingredients from sustainable farms. This style of **irori** ("sunken hearth") cooking is based on folklore — it is believed that olden-day samurais in the region skewered their vegetables and river fish using their swords and cooked the ingredients over an open fire. **Irori** sunken hearths are installed at each table at the Nitsuite restaurant.

Dinner is plentiful and delicious, beginning with a few appetizing starters; followed by multiple plates of sashimi, meat, iwana river fish and vegetable skewers roasted at the **irori**; and concluding with a **nabe** miso stew with pork, regional rice cooked in onsen water, and seasonal dessert. The nutritious Japanese-style breakfast might include steamed vegetables and meats cooked using Kamimoku Onsen water; handmade tofu made with organic soybeans from Oze in Gunma; natto beans; grilled fish; and miso soup.

THE TAKEAWAY

My experience at Tatsumikan was not a lavish one, but the sincere and down-to-earth hospitality offered by Fukatsu and his team made me feel right at home.

Before my departure, Fukatsu actually brought out Kyoshi Yamashita's original collage, which he miraculously was in possession of and had been safekeeping for many years, to share with me. The collage was created using the Chigiri-e method of assembling pieces of torn colored paper.

I was very touched by Fukatsu's kindness in sharing Tatsumikan's precious asset with me.

Minakami offers a variety of outdoor activities for each of the four seasons. In spring, summer and autumn, cherry and strawberry picking, firefly watching, trekking, water rafting and other adventure sports are all popular. During the winter season, there are nine ski resorts in the region for skiing and snowboarding.

ONSEN WATER

Type: A combination of Chloride and Sulphate Springs (with sodium, calcium elements)

Color and Odor: Colorless; odorless

pH: 7.9

Gensen Kakenagashi: Yes

Filtered and Circulated: No

Temperature at Source: 40°C

Temperature at Bath: 41°C

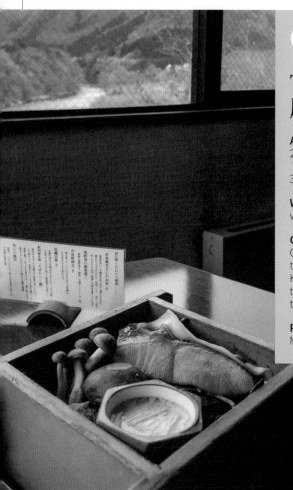

Tatsumikan
辰巳館

Address
2052 Kamimoku, Minakami,
Tone, Gunma Prefecture,
379-1303 | +81 278-72-3055

Website
www.tatsumikan.com

Getting Here
Convenient. From Tokyo Station, take
the Joetsu Line Shinkansen to Jomo-
Kogen station (1hr15min); then take
the free hotel shuttle bus at the station
to Tatsumikan (reserve in advance).

Price Range / Rooms
Mid-range. Traditional Japanese style.

Bettei Senjuan, Gunma Prefecture

谷川温泉

別邸 仙寿庵

THE STORY

Nestled at the foot of Mount Tanigawa in the town of Minakami, Bettei Senjuan is an award-winning high-end contemporary Japanese ryokan. It has been a member of the Relais & Chateaux since 2012, and is most well-known for its architectural design and culinary offerings. Senjuan is easily accessible by Shinkansen from Tokyo, making it one of the best city escapes. Minakami town offers a variety of outdoor activities all year round, from rafting to canyoning, trekking and skiing.

Founder Tomio Kubo opened Senjuan in 1997. He is also the owner of Ryokan Tanigawa, a more traditional Japanese inn adjacent to Senjuan. Senjuan is based on Kubo's vision of offering traditional Japanese hospitality in a modern and deluxe setting. Senjuan is currently run by Kubo's son, Hidehiro Kubo.

THE DESIGN

Senjuan was built over 83,000 square meters of land in a quiet forest. The stunning curved glass corridor is the ryokan's signature design, standing 8 meters high and stretching 40 meters long. The tall floor-to-ceiling windows offer remarkable views of Mount Tanigawa — it's particularly stunning when this mountain is capped in snow on a clear winter day. The interiors are tasteful and throught-provoking: an Edo-style ink wall; and handcrafted **washi** paper kumiko (traditional lattice woodwork) doors are just a few of the interesting touches. The natural color tone used by the ryokan gives it a Zen, calming effect.

There are only 18 rooms in Senjuan, and all of them are Japanese and western style, paired with gorgeous views of Mount Tanigawa. Elegant, extremely spacious and nicely decorated with Japanese paintings and artwork, some rooms even come with a moon-viewing deck.

THE WATER

Senjuan has a private bath in every guest room, but a big gender-separated communal bath is also on the premises. The clear odorless onsen water is extracted from three sources nearby, then piped to the baths at Senjuan. The two outdoor **rotenburo** baths, the Suzumushi no Yu（すずむしの湯）and Hotaru no Yu（ほたるの湯）, sit by the Tanigawa River and the adjacent forest — both baths are lined with natural stones that help to maintain water quality and temperatures. The slightly alkaline onsen water is maintained at around 41 degrees Celsius and contains natural minerals like sodium, calcium, and sulfate, which are said to improve circulation, aid digestion and moisturize the skin.

THE CUISINE

Dining at Senjuan is an over-the-top experience. Master chef Anzai Susumu whips up Gunma delicacies using exemplary culinary techniques and an artistic flourish. All ingredients are carefully selected, without synthetic seasoning or preservatives added. The premium-quality utensils are hand-picked by the owner and staff from across Japan.

Guests would dine in the restaurant's private dining rooms, and no two dining rooms are alike. Dinner is a succession of delicate dishes, starting with Japanese amuse-bouches and followed by sashimi, seasonal seafoods and vegetables, grilled meats, rice, and sweets to wrap up the meal. The **kaiseki** feast is unforgettable and creative — think uni (sea urchin) jelly topped with eggplant mousse, a rare yet delightful mix of flavors and textures. To enhance the overall dining experience, Senjuan has a comprehensive list of western and Japanese wines to accompany the delicious meal. Remember to sample Senjuan's amazing umeshu (plum wine) collection from distilleries across Japan.

THE TAKEAWAY

At Senjuan, the flawless execution of traditional Japanese hospitality in a contemporary setting redefined the ryokan experience for me. I felt revitalized by the healing waters, the exquisite cuisine, the tranquility, and the attention to beautiful details here. It was also wonderful to be able to sample from exactly 100 types of umeshu on offer at Senjuan — it was pure paradise for someone like me, who has a soft spot for plum wine.

Bettei Senjuan
別邸 仙寿庵

Address
614 Tanigawa, Minakami, Tone, Gunma Prefecture , 379-1619 | +81 278-20-4141

Website
www.senjyuan.jp

Getting Here
Convenient. From Tokyo Station, take the Joetsu Shinkansen to Jomo-Kogen Station (1hr15min), then take a taxi or a pre-arranged free shuttle to Bettei Senjuan (20min).

Price Range / Rooms
High-end. Traditional Japanese and western style.

ONSEN WATER

Type: A combination of Sulfate and Chloride Springs (with sodium elements)

Color and Odor: Clear; odorless

pH: 8.4

Gensen Kakenagashi: Yes

Filtered and Circulated: No

Temperature at Source: Unknown

Temperature at Bath: 41.4°C

Hatcho no Yu, Tochigi Prefecture

奥鬼怒温泉

八丁の湯

THE STORY

Deeply hidden in a 1,300-meter-high mountain in Okukinu Onsen village, Tochigi Prefecture, Hatcho no Yu sits among an unspoiled beech forest within Nikko National Park. This ryokan is quite out of reach — it is not accessible by public transport, and private cars are restricted from entering the national park. The only entry is via the ryokan-provided shuttle bus.

Although it is isolated, there is no lack of customers at Hatcho no Yo, especially during the month of October, when the tree leaves start to change into their autumn colors.

Hatcho no Yu first opened its doors in 1929, owned by a man named Tomijiro Suzuki. Suzuki discovered a natural hot spring source in the vicinity and he subsequently bought the land on which to build a traditional Japanese guesthouse. There was no electricity here until 1988, and no proper roads before the area was registered as a part of the Nikko National Park. Harsh winter weather also makes maintenance at Hatcho no Yu particularly difficult.

THE DESIGN

The building consists of 25 rooms in total, with traditional **tatami**-matted Japanese-style accommodations in the original main building, and western-style log houses in the new extended section of the inn — an unusual feature for Japanese lodgings. These beautiful log houses were completely handcrafted from large, round, heat-retaining Canadian timbers that can withstand heavy snow, giving the interiors a homely ambience.

In 2013, the current owner, Jun Oguri, purchased Hatcho no Yu from Suzuki to continue the legend of this secluded inn. Oguri has upgraded the inn with modern amenities, including western-style beds and contemporary furnishings. Wife Keiko Oguri is the ryokan's **okami**, and she works together with her husband to take care of the inn's daily operations.

THE WATER

Bathing in the **rotenburo** at Hacho no Yu is the most remarkable experience. There are four **yatenburo** (野天風呂 , open-air baths in the wild) options here; these natural pools sit right in the middle of the wild forest, facing a waterfall. The Yukimi no Yu (雪見の湯), Takimi no Yu (滝見の湯) and Shakunage no Yu (石楠花の湯) are **konyoku** offerings, while the Takimi Rotenburo (滝見露天風呂) is for women only.

Female bathers can wrap themselves in towels while using the mixed-gender baths. The unfiltered thermal water is rich in minerals like iron, sodium and calcium, which may appear in the form of floating white cotton-like deposits called **yunohana**. The hot spring water comes from sources nearby that range from 43 to 51 degrees Celsius in temperature depending on the time of year. The water is then naturally cooled to 40 to 43 degrees Celsius. This type of natural-wilderness onsen bathing is indeed a rare find in Japan.

THE CUISINE

Dinner at Hatcho no Yu is all about Tochigi Prefecture's wild mountain treasures: think meat, seafood and vegetables. The feast begins in the dining hall, with **yuba**, konnyaku (konjac), and grated yam appetizers; followed by dishes like grilled iwana fish, and yashiomasu (freshwater rainbow trout fed on olive oil) sashimi. The wild boar **nabe** and Japanese beef sukiyaki are the most popular dishes with guests. Rice is sourced from a local Tochigi farm and cooked in pure mountain water.

Hatcho no Yu
八丁の湯

Address
857 Kawamata, Nikko, Tochigi Prefecture, 321-2717 | +81 288-96-0306

Website
www.8tyo-no-yu.co.jp

Getting Here
Remote. By private car from Tokyo: Drive to Meotobuchi Parking at Okukinu in Tochigi Prefecture (3.5hrs). Leave your car at the parking lot and take the shuttle bus to Hatcho no Yu (reserve in advance). By public transport: Take the JR Limited Express train "Spacia" from Tokyo to Kinugawa Onsen Station (120min), then transfer to the Nikko Municipal Bus towards Meotobuchi (100min). Take the ryokan's pre-arranged shuttle bus to Hatcho no Yu.

Price Range / Rooms
Affordable. Traditional Japanese or western style.

ONSEN WATER

Type: A combination of Chloride and Bicarbonate Springs (with sodium elements)

Color and Odor: Clear; odorless

pH: 8.4

Gensen Kakenagashi: Yes

Filtered and Circulated: No

Temperature at Source: 43°C to 51°C

Temperature at Bath: 40°C to 43°C

THE TAKEAWAY

Visiting Hatcho no Yu is certainly a luxurious treatment for the senses. Making my way to the inn was so exciting, as the shuttle bus wound through the beech forest's narrow roads. I was warmly welcomed by Oguri-san upon arrival, and she spent an hour with me to share the story of Hatcho no Yu.

Nothing can beat bathing in the **yatenburo**, as I let my mind completely immerse itself in nature. It was such a delight to sit in the Takimi no Yu onsen pool, enshrouded in the unspoiled forest, as I listened to the rush of the waterfall and admired the multi-colored forest. Soaking up all of the supposed therapeutic benefits of the hot spring, I found comfort in this soothing setting. It was truly a blessing to be able to spend quality time in such a natural environment.

Hoshino Resorts KAI Nikko, Tochigi Prefecture

中禅寺温泉

星野リゾート 界日光

THE STORY

In the historical town of Nikko in the Tochigi Prefecture, where centuries-old Shinto and Buddhist shrines attract many tourists year round, lies KAI Nikko. It is a tranquil, contemporary Japanese ryokan at the foot of the sacred Mount Nantai.

Nikko is regarded as a sacred town, with a long history that dates back to the Nara period in the 8th century, when monk Shodo established the Rinnoji temple there. Nikko became a significant town during the Edo period, when the Toshogu Shrine was constructed in memory of the powerful shogun Tokugawa Ieyasu. Toshogu and other Nikko shrines are designated National Treasures of Japan as well as UNESCO World Heritage Sites.

KAI is the brainchild of Japan's leading luxury hotel group Hoshino Resorts, offering an authentic onsen experience, top-notch hospitality, and artistic cuisine designed to reflect the cultural uniqueness of the location. Since opening in 2014, KAI Nikko has been receiving not only Japanese visitors, but also international travelers. The attentive English-speaking staff makes communication a breeze.

Cultural activities are available on site. For example, every evening after dinner, the Nikko **geta** dance — a local traditional tap dance — is performed by staff wearing traditional Edo-period straw sandals. Guests are also invited to go on stage during this time.

THE DESIGN

The ryokan is nestled on the eastern shore of Lake Chuzenji. The refurbished building is inspired by the history and heritage of Nikko and successfully infuses traditional elements into its interior design.

The pampering experience at KAI begins with a glass of champagne and some welcome sweets at the Woodcraft Library. A dedicated staff member would then lead you to your room to introduce the facilities and services available at the hotel.

Rooms are elegantly styled, with most of them boasting views of Lake Chuzenji. The KAI Signature Room is the nicest of them all, featuring traditional kumiko (traditional lattice woodwork) art by local Nikko carpenters. Comfortable beds and soothing lights promise a restful night's sleep.

THE WATER

The simple alkaline spring waters at KAI Nikko are sourced from Nikko Wanoshiro Onsen, and are said to help with muscular pain, frozen shoulders and chronic gastrointestinal diseases. The soothing water is kept at around 40 to 42 degrees Celsius and is piped from the source to the gender-separated common baths, each with indoor and outdoor bath pools that are lined with aromatic cedar and rock.

To preserve a very special ancient Nikko tradition, a bucket of Japanese sake from the Futarasan Shinto Shrine is poured into the steaming waters at a designated time every morning and evening. Bathing with sake water is believed to help one recover from fatigue, among other benefits.

THE CUISINE

The cuisine at KAI Nikko makes for a classic, memorable experience. Dishes are meticulously prepared by the head chef and his team and artfully presented to each guest at the restaurant or private banquet rooms. The staff provides a detailed explanation of the making of each dish in English for foreign customers, and an English menu is also available. The food is plated onto beautiful ceramic tableware graced with colorful paintings of famous historical Nikko elements.

Dinner begins with Nikko-style **yuba**. It is delicate and soft, topped with sea urchin and refreshing stock jelly. Assorted seasonal delicacies follow. The main courses include a "Millefeuille" **yuba shabu shabu** with slices of Japanese wagyu beef and tofu skin; and a sizzling wagyu beef grilled on ōya (heatproof igneous stones found in Nikko's rock mines). And finally, guests can enjoy fusion-style desserts like a hojicha (roasted green tea) crème brûlée, **yuba** mousse, or cheese soufflé.

ONSEN WATER

Type: Simple Spring

Color and Odor: Clear; odorless

pH: 9.5

Gensen Kakenagashi: No

Filtered and Circulated: Unknown

Temperature at Source: 39.4°C

Temperature at Bath: 41°C

Hoshino Resorts KAI Nikko
星野リゾート
界 日光

Address:
2482-1 Chugu, Nikko, Tochigi Prefecture, 321-1661 | +81-50-3786-1144

Website
kai-ryokan.jp

Getting Here
Remote. KAI Nikko offers a free shuttle bus from Tokyo Station that takes you directly to KAI Nikko during the winter season, from December to March. Or take the JR Limited Express trains from Shinjuku Station in Tokyo to Tobu Nikko Station (2hrs), then hop on the Tobu Bus to the Chuzenji Onsen bus stop (40min), where there are free shuttle buses to the hotel.

Price Range / Rooms
High-end. Japanese and western style.

THE TAKEAWAY

Lake Chuzenji has enchanting seasonal views that take your breath away. I was completely captivated by my surroundings during a chilly November stay. Too late for the fiery colors of the autumn foliage and too early for the snowy white scenes of winter, time seemed to stand still when I sat by the large windows in my room, which overlooked the pristine lake and the mountains. The stillness of the lake, the clarity of the sky and the bareness of the trees formed a solitary scene that I could stare at for hours. Some days the views were clear and bright, while other days the mood was romantic and mysterious, with a sky covered in fog and low-hanging clouds.

Nikko boasts 1,200 years of history, and a number of worthy sights. A day visit to the extraordinary Toshogu Shrine is a must: this national treasure consists of 42 structures that were built in 1617. The lavish ornaments and exquisite carpentry work found at the shrine contain both Buddhist and Shinto elements that are rare to find in Japan. Another landmark is the Rinnoji, an ancient Buddhist temple near the Toshogu Shrine.

Meigetsuso, Yamagata Prefecture

名月荘 上山温泉

THE STORY

Located in the historical Kaminoyama Onsen town in Yamagata Prefecture, and with charming Mount Zao as backdrop, Meigetsuso is a quintessential boutique ryokan that is highly regarded for its attentive service. It is a member of the Yado Authentic Japanese Resorts, a Japanese organization that fosters and promotes Japanese inns dedicated to local tradition and modern luxury.

Meigetsuso literally means "harvest moon inn". The different phases of the moon can be appreciated from the ryokan as it rises above the Zao mountains. This elegant venue has earned many loyal customers and is consistently ranked as a top ryokan in the area. Its management style is unlike that of large hotel chains; Meigetsuso offers a more distinct and personalized service.

Founder Toshiyuki Kikuchi decided to remodel and rename a western-style hotel that he inherited from his father, and the hotel was converted into a two-story Japanese-style inn, even though this type of architecture was against the popular high-rise buildings of the time. In 1996, Meigetsuso moved to the current forested address, on a spacious piece of land that allowed for Kikuchi's pursuit of creating a sukiya-style (villa-like, tea house-inspired building) single-story ryokan. Kikuchi's son, Tomonobu Kikuchi, has since taken the helm at Meigetsuso. Tomonobu Kikuchi grew up in Meigetuso and has assisted his father since he was young. His wife, Masako Kikuchi, is the ryokan's **okami**. Mrs. Kikuchi would gracefully greet guests in her elegant kimono every day, and she also speaks fluent English.

THE DESIGN

The inn's décor is tasteful and classic, an intriguing merge of Japanese and western elements. You will see both rare antique pieces and contemporary furniture displayed together. Also worth mentioning is the unique collection of designer chairs found throughout the single-story building.

There are only 20 guest rooms in Meigetsuso, and each room is a one-story detached villa featuring a peaceful garden. All of the rooms are connected by one long indoor hallway. The warmly lit and spacious rooms feature a blend of western and Japanese elements, such as a **tatami**-matted living room with **washi** screen doors, and a separate dining area. Each room is unique — no two are the same.

THE WATER

Kaminoyama is an old onsen town with half-a-millennium of history to its name. Legend has it that a 15th-century monk saw a crane recover from its injuries after bathing in the hot springs of Kaminoyama. A stone statue of a crane can be found in the town center, which is believed to be the birthplace of Kaminoyama's original onsen source.

At Meigetsuso, the gender-separated communal baths have both indoor and outdoor onsen pools that face an inner garden. The soft alkaline water contains sodium and calcium, and is cooled to a pleasant temperature of 41 degrees Celsius from a much higher source temperature, by adding mineral-rich natural well water to the mix. This type of water is said to help with alleviating muscular pain and fatigue.

For a more private soak, the 17 villas come with in-room indoor or outdoor baths, using the same high-quality onsen water. There are also two other baths available for private use, including an open-air mountain-facing family bath made from a hollowed-out rock from Mount Zao; and an especially deep bath that requires users to stand up while soaking.

THE CUISINE

A highlight at Meigetsuso is its sumptuous **kaiseki** dinner offering. The multi-course meal is a showcase of Yamagata's bountiful produce, from both land and sea. Head chef Katsutoshi Kimura creates heart-stopping, memorable dishes that showcase the flavors of the entire prefecture. Dishes are precisely prepared and beautifully decorated, according to the seasons of the year. A few outstanding dishes include the oyster with fried yam; the citrus-pickled radish with dashi broth; the grilled Yonezawa marbled wagyu beef steak; and the sweet and tasty snow crab. Each dish is complemented by a side of locally grown vegetables.

The meals are served in the guest rooms by English-speaking staff, who take care to explain details like what ingredients are used, and how the dishes are prepared and cooked.

Meigetsuso's in-house handmade udon absolutely needs a mention — the flat, wide and bouncy noodles have been served at the ryokan for more than 22 years. Meigetsuso's cellar boasts a great selection of Yamagata **nihonshu** and wines from both local and international wineries.

Meigetsuso
名月荘

Address
50 Hayama, Kaminoyama, Yamagata Prefecture, 999-3242 | +81 23-672-0330

Website
www.meigetsuso.co.jp

Getting Here
Convenient. Take Yamagata Shinkansen Line from Tokyo Station to Kaminoyama Onsen Station (2.5hrs).

Price Range / Rooms
High-end. Traditional Japanese style.

THE TAKEAWAY

Built within a forest, Meigetsuso makes nature appreciation an integral part of the experience. A stroll in the serene Fairy Forest nearby helps to clear the mind. **Okami** Masako Kikuchi took me on a tour around the ryokan, and I learned about her and her husband's commitment to never stop making improvements and enhancements at Meigetsuso. Their goal is to create a tranquil environment that offers an instant relief from life's daily stresses.

There are plenty of quiet public spaces and tranquil corners at Meigetsuso. I liked having some private me-time at the lounge by the lobby, which is tastefully decorated and perfect for some after-bath relaxation. Being able to lie on one of the designer couches while listening to some lighthearted jazz music was simply a divine experience.

ONSEN WATER

Type: A combination of Sulfate and Chloride Springs (with sodium, calcium elements)

Color and Odor: Clear; odorless

pH: 8.2

Gensen Kakenagashi: No

Filtered and Circulated: No

Temperature at Source: 65°C

Temperature at Bath: 41°C

Yamado, Iwate Prefecture

湯川温泉

山人

THE STORY

Situated in Iwate Prefecture near the border of Akita, Yamado, a contemporary boutique onsen resort, can be found in the tranquil mountains of Nishiwaga Yugawa Onsen town. The ryokan fuses Japan's centuries-old customs with modernized services and accommodations. Yamado staff are attentive, friendly and professional.

Staying at this mountain sanctuary is a retreat for all the senses, and purification of the senses is indeed what most mountain worshippers and forest bathers come to seek. Yamado's secluded location allows one to focus on the sights and sounds of nature, from the running river to the chirping birds, the tranquil forest, the sweet crisp air, and the soothing Yugawa hot spring.

Yamado literally means "mountain people", a name for local experts with profound knowledge of the nearby peaks. The aptly named ryokan is run by proprietor Masaaki Koutaka. After finishing university in Tokyo, he returned to Iwate, his hometown, in the 1980s to take charge of family-run Ryokan Suehiro situated nearby. He then spent 20 years to create his dream resort — and the story of Yamado began in 2009.

Running this mountain resort with Koutaka is wife and Chief Operations Manager Yoshie Koutaka. Daughter Maki Koutaka has also returned to Iwate to help with the family business.

THE DESIGN

Yamado's structure is built to align with the original terrain, without disturbing its natural topography. The building was designed to withstand heavy snowfall in the region. With only 12 spacious western-style suites to accommodate guests, privacy is pretty much a guarantee.

Rooms are cozy and tastefully designed, with comfortable western-style beds. The Seizanro suites are maisonettes located in the upper part of the hill, while the Rokkabo and Rokujubo suites are single-story, with a river-viewing deck for the enjoyment of the splendid scenery outside.

THE WATER

Yamado offers luxurious relaxation at the Yuba Issun (湯場一寸) **rotenburo**. This open-air bath offers captivating views of mountain streams and majestic forests for guests' private enjoyment. The clear alkaline waters are sodium chloride sulfate-based, transparent, and odorless.

The water is said to help with alleviating dry skin, boosting circulation, and healing cuts and burns. The hot spring at the source, which is around 51.4 degrees Celsius, is piped to the tub, then cooled naturally to body-friendly temperatures and undiluted. It's an absolute thrill to soak in this natural aqua pool under a frosty winter sky.

Unlike most Japanese lodgings, there is no communal bath at Yamado. Each room comes with its own shower facilities and private indoor bath, with onsen water feeding directly from the spring source.

THE CUISINE

Dining at Yamado is an exquisite journey, leveraging both Japanese and western cooking techniques. At restaurant Fukuzenbo, experience a farm-to-table procession of gourmet delicacies featuring distinctive produce found in Iwate and Akita regions. Executive chef Shigeru Shibata works wonders on his dishes, which are visually appealing and exceptionally delicious.

Dinner begins with mixed raw greens freshly picked from Yamado's own farm, served with a homemade iwana fish-based dipping sauce that has been warmed over candle fire. Next in line are assorted appetizers, including Iwate shorthorn beef slow-cooked in Yamado's onsen water; broiled and marinated iwana fish; and buckwheat from Nishiwaga mountain, cooked in nameko mushroom dashi stock. To cleanse the palate before the main dishes arrive, pickled daikon (white radish) pieces are brought to the table. This winter treat is harvested in advance and preserved with salt and vinegar.

One main dish is a roasted honey chicken from Yamado's own poultry farm. The staff spent seven years at a renowned chicken farm in Miyazaki Prefecture to pick up a special slow-growth breeding technique to nurture their animals.

Roasted Hakkinton (aka platinum) pork is another signature. The famed pork from Hanamaki town is cooked sous-vide and then roasted, making the meat extremely tender, fragrant and melt-in-your-mouth. The culinary journey ends with a dessert of ice cream pastry.

You'll wake up to a healthy Japanese-style breakfast of tofu and vegetable **nabe** simmered in freshly handmade local soy milk; pickled vegetables; grilled fish; locally grown rice; and onsen tamago (soft-poached egg).

Yamado
山人

Address
52 Chiwari, 71-10 Yugawa, Nishiwaga, Waga, Iwate Prefecture, 029-5514 | +81 197-82-2222

Website
www.yamado.co.jp

Getting Here
Remote. By Air: Fly from Tokyo Haneda Airport to Akita Airport (1hr). Drive from Akita Airport to Yamado (1.5hrs). By Train: From Tokyo Station, take the JR Tohoku Shinkansen Line to Kitakami Station (2.5hrs), then transfer to the JR Kitakami Line express train to get to Hottoyuda Station. Then take taxi to Yamado (7min).

Price Range / Rooms
High-end. Contemporary Japanese style.

THE TAKEAWAY

It was early December and freezing when I arrived. Heavy snowfall turned the area into a winter wonderland within a couple of hours. The scene was remarkably beautiful, stunning. I quietly and solemnly admired the winter scenery for hours on end. I made my way to the steamy **rotenburo**, my body first shivering in the frozen air, then enveloped by the warm onsen water. Snowflakes fell on my bare head, and my heart leapt in silent joy.

Masaaki and Yoshie Koutaka sent me off the next frosty morning, waving goodbye until I could barely see them in my car. Staying at Yamado is indeed a treat for all the senses. I left feeling well-pampered, well-fed and lovingly served. I'd gladly return.

ONSEN WATER

Type: A combination of Chloride and Sulfate Springs (with sodium elements)

Color and Odor: Clear; odorless

pH: 7.6

Gensen Kakenagashi: Yes

Filtered and Circulated: No

Temperature at Source: 51.4°C

Temperature at Bath: 45°C

Tsuru no Yu, Akita Prefecture

乳頭温泉

鶴の湯

THE STORY

Tsuru no Yu is an unrefined traditional inn, which sets it apart from the others included in this book. Unlike a typical modern Japanese ryokan that features meticulous hospitality, delicate meals and elegant accommodations, Tsuru no Yu offers no such luxuries. Yet it continues to find itself at the top of the hot spring top lists, and is frequently featured in the media. It is also fully booked throughout the year and reservations generally need to be made no less than six months in advance. But once you're in, Tsuru no Yu offers an exceptional old-Japan countryside experience.

As the longest-standing ryokan in Nyuto Onsen town, with a rich history that dates back to the late 1600s, Tsuru no Yu is surrounded by a beech forest at the southern tip of the Towada Hachimantai National Park in Akita Prefecture. It is isolated from the six other lodgings in the area, tucked deep in the mountains, and is only reachable via a 3-kilometer narrow gravel road. Reservations are accepted strictly by phone, and there is no network coverage and only limited WiFi on the premises.

Current proprietor Kazushi Sato only gained the management rights to Tsuru no Yu in 1983, when the 13th-generation owner had no family members to pass the business onto. It was a costly endeavor for Sato to repair the decaying Tsuru no Yu once he became the new owner, and there were stretches of up to six months when not a single customer would visit. Sato only encountered success after many years of hardwork.

THE DESIGN

At Tsuru no Yu, remnants of the Edo period can still be seen. Sato resisted the idea of modernizing the inn and its surrounding areas, but worked instead to make restorations that would leave everything as intact as possible.

The wooden huts, built more than 100 years ago, feature steep thatch straw roofs. The unpolished wooden gates that lead to the unpaved walkway are lined with these ancient-looking huts, taking one back to a different, old-timey era. The decor is straightforward and practical; the

THE WATER

Tsuru no Yu literally means "hot water of cranes" — it is said that the ryokan was given its name after some injured cranes healing their wounds by the soothing **yu** were spotted by hunters.

Public bathing at Tsuru no Yu was recorded as early as 400 years ago. Today, Tsuru no Yu is consistently ranked as one of the most desirable secluded hot springs in Japan, attracting locals as well as visitors each year to its legendary milky white **rotenburo** baths. Some guests even

come for week-long **toji** (湯治, hot spring therapy) retreats.

There are four different spring sources at Tsuru no Yu: the Shirayu (白湯), Kuroyu (黒湯), Nakanoyu (中の湯) and Takinoyu (滝の湯). These sources feed water into the five indoor and outdoor baths, all of which consist of different water compositions. Out of all the baths, the most famous one is the **konyoku rotenburo** (mixed-gender open-air bath). This open-air bath is irregularly shaped and quite large in size, doors and furniture are unpolished and misaligned. But it is the ryokan's rustic simplicity and imperfections that give it a sophisticated charm and a down-to-earth vibe. Tsuru no Yu was designated as a Registered Tangible Cultural Property by the Japanese Government in 2010.

There are 36 rooms altogether, all traditional Japanese **tatami**-matted. The more spacious rooms at the Honjin (本陣) main wing come with an **irori**, and the rooms at the annexes are smaller and more basic. Prices are extremely reasonable at Tsuru no Yu.

and one side of the pool is partially covered by a wooden shelter that is supported by crooked trunks and branches. The onsen water bubbles up from the bottom of the tub at a comfortable temperature of 41 to 43 degrees Celsius. The water at the source is almost transparent, but turns extremely white and opaque once the minerals in the water come in contact with air.

This popular **konyoku** did not exist when Sato first inherited the ryokan from its previous owner. Completely by coincidence, water miraculously gushed out from the

grounds where repair work was being done on site, which gave birth to this onsen pool. Known as a **jifunsen** (natural pressure artesian spring), this type of onsen is extremely rare in Japan and only makes up 1 percent of all hot springs in the country.

There is also the Oshira no Yu (大白の湯), a women-only open-air **jifunsen** complete with bubbling water, for those who might find mixed-gender baths intimidating. The bath is large in size and the water is said to help improve fertility.

THE CUISINE

Food at Tsuru no Yu is nothing fancy. Dinner is served in the rooms for those staying at the Honjin, and at the dining hall for annex guests. Everyone sits cross-legged or kneels on the **tatami**-matted floor. A small tray that holds several stews, sansai (mountain vegetables), and grilled iwana fish is placed right in front of the guests.

Tsuru no Yu's very own yama no imo **nabe** (a hearty hotpot filled with yam balls, homemade miso, pork, and plenty of wildly grown vegetables and mountain mushrooms, all cooked above burning charcoal in the **irori**) is a guest favorite. It is best enjoyed with some local Akita sake.

Tsuru no Yu
鶴の湯

Address:
50 Kokuyurin, Sendatsuizawa, Tazawa, Semboku, Akita Prefecture, 014-1204 | +81 187-46-2139

Website
www.tsurunoyu.com

Getting Here
Remote. Fly from Tokyo Haneda to Akita Airport, then drive directly to the ryokan (2hrs). Also reachable by Shinkansen (Akita Shinkansen Line) from Tokyo Station to Tazawako Station (3hrs). There are regular buses (Nyuto Line) from Tazawako Station to Alpa Komakusa Station (45min). Tsuru no Yu can arrange free shuttle bus pick up from Alpa Komakusa (reserve by phone in advance).

Price Range / Rooms
Affordable. Traditional Japanese style.

ONSEN WATER

Type: Shirayu: A combination of Chloride and Bicarbonate Springs (with sodium elements) | Kuroyu, Nakanoyu, Takinoyu: A combination of Sulfur, Chloride and Bicarbonate Springs (with sodium, calcium elements)

Color and Odor: Opaque white; mildly sulfurous

pH: 6.6 to 7.1

Gensen Kakenagashi: Yes

Filtered and Circulated: No

Temperature at Source: 43°C to 51°C

Temperature at Bath: 40°C to 43°C

THE TAKEAWAY

Dipping in the steaming waters in a picturesque postcard setting is an absolutely surreal experience — Tsuru no Yu has got to be one of the best onsen experiences I have ever had. The scenery was beyond beautiful; it was simply mind-blowing. Time suddenly stood still while I bathed in the heavenly waters, conversing with guests from different parts of the world. Everyone there had the same goal: to have a soak in this super-secret onsen. Don't come for a day trip: Tsuru no Yu's true charms cannot be fully appreciated without staying for a night or two.

Lamp no Yado Aoni Onsen, Aomori Prefecture

青荷温泉

ランプの宿 青荷温泉

THE STORY

The Tohoku region remains somewhat untouched and mysterious even to this day. On the northern end lies Aomori Prefecture, home to "Aomori Nebuta Matsuri", one of Japan's biggest annual festivals. Taking inspiration from folklore and mythical legends, this special summer festival sees vibrant-colored, exotic-figured giant floating lanterns crafted by local experts being paraded through the town each year.

There are still pockets of Aomori where scenes of old Japan can be found. In the town of Kuroishi, near the Hachimantai mountains, an unusual Japanese inn called Lamp no Yado Aoni Onsen sits in a beautiful gorge next to the Aoni River. Although rather out of reach, the ryokan is a must for those seeking a one-of-a-kind experience.

There are more than 200 kerosene-fueled lamps at Aoni Onsen — but no electricity, television or data networks are available here. One is encouraged to completely detach from the hustle of urban living and simply dial back to the basics during their stay.

The road leading to Aoni Onsen is rough and unpaved, winding through a narrow mountain passage. There are signs that say "Aoni Onsen" along the way, but besides these clues hinting at civilization, one might as well be in complete wilderness.

Opening the ryokan's sliding wooden entrance reveals the ryokan's old-world charms. Oil lamps are hung from the reception hall's high ceiling; a big painting of mythical gods graces the wall, showcasing Aomori's distinctive arts culture.

Aoni was established in 1929 by disabled Japanese poet Niwa Yogaku, who fell in love with the landscape and wrote a series of poems titled "Aoni Gorge" in tribute. Yogaku spent six years building the lodge. Atsuhisa Harada is the seventh-generation owner; he took over the ryokan in 2011. Harada abandoned city life in Tokyo and moved to Aomori for some simple countryside living. The humble owner is usually found at the reception desk assisting customers.

THE DESIGN

The accommodations at Aoni Onsen are basic. Most guest rooms are located in the two-story main building, and come with traditional **tatami** floors and shared bathrooms in the hallway. You won't find extravagant amenities here, but rather, simple architecture and creaky wooden floors. Guests even have to make their own futon beds at night. Yet the rooms are neat and simple, and most offer views of the rich forested land and charming waterways nearby. There are no power outlets in the rooms: one oil lamp is delivered to each room every evening. The building uses a minimum amount of generator-powered electricity to satisfy fire and safety regulations.

THE WATER

The original hot spring at Aoni was discovered long ago. But there were no proper roads at the time and no one had the directions to this hidden onsen. Today, there are four baths scattered in the onsen's vicinity, and all are **gensen kakenagashi** — meaning 100 percent of the water comes straight from the source, and nothing else is added. Onsen water oozes up at about 47 to 48 degrees Celsius and is then naturally cooled down. There is no shower facility at any of the baths — instead, one washes the body with scoops of warm natural spring water before dipping into the bath pools.

Right next to the entrance is indoor bath Kenroku no Yu (健六の湯). This gender-separated bath sits inside a wooden hut that is completely made from hiba (Japanese cypress), with floor-to-ceiling timber-framed large windows. In the morning, sunbeams penetrate through the windows and reflect on the steamy waters, resulting in a truly magical scene.

Behind the main building is the stone-lined **konyoku rotenburo** Takimi no Yu (滝見の湯). **Konyoku** is a rarity in modern Japan, but a few can still be found in the Tohoku region. Twice daily and for an hour at a time, the Taikimi no Yu is for women's use only.

THE CUISINE

Dinner is served at the dimly lamp-lit Ohiroma dining hall. Guests are encouraged to sit cross-legged on the **tatami** floors. The chef comes in to sing a thanks-giving song before dinner begins. The food here is simple and hearty, using freshly harvested ingredients from the nearby river and mountainside. Think appetizers of pickled vegetables and kelp; stuffed tofu pouches; fried chicken; wild greens stew; and a classic **nabe** of local boar simmered in broth. You can help yourself with unlimited rice and miso soup, or a chargrilled iwana fish seasoned with sea salt, cooked over an **irori**. Dinner at Aoni is always a night to remember — dining under the soft glow of oil lamps is irresistibly romantic.

THE TAKEAWAY

Time seemed to pass much slower in the stillness of Aoni's tranquil surrounds — I felt it was a perfect time to connect with family and friends in the cozy setting. It was strangely romantic to catch the gentle flames from the lamps dancing in the darkness. The quietness allowed me to pay more attention to the beautiful details around me.

A night's stay at Aoni Onsen is pure inspiration — it taught me the art of minimalism, for one. I was also able to practice sustainable living and be creative with nature's offerings. It was indeed a forgotten luxury to be doing absolutely nothing here. I allowed my mind to completely switch off, spending a quiet night in exile — free of noise, stress, news, and social media.

Aoni Onsen might not be the right ryokan for everyone, but those who stay with an open heart would agree that the experience is one-of-a-kind.

📍

Lamp no Yado
Aoni Onsen
ランプの宿 青荷温泉

Address
1-7 Aonisawa, Okiura, Kuroishi, Aomori
Prefecture, 036-0402 | +81 172-54-8588

Website
aoninet.com

Getting Here
Remote. By train: From Tokyo Station, take the
Tohoku Shinkansen to Shin-Aomori Station
(3.5hrs), then transfer to the JR Ou Main Line train
to Hirosaki Station. Take the Konan Tetsudo-
Konan Line to Kuroishi Station. Then take a local
bus to Nijino Lake; free Aoni Onsen shuttle buses
are available. By air and car: Fly from Tokyo
Haneda Airport to Aomori Airport (1hr), then drive
from Aomori Airport to Aoni Onsen (1hr).

Price Range / Rooms
Affordable. Traditional Japanese style.

ONSEN
WATER

Type: Simple Spring

Color and Odor: Clear; odorless

pH: 7.8

Gensen Kakenagashi: Yes

Filtered and Circulated: No

Temperature at Source:
47.3°C to 48.1°C

Temperature at Bath: 40°C to 42°C

Takinoya, Hokkaido Prefecture

登別温泉

滝乃家

THE STORY

In the phenomenal onsen town of Noboribetsu, visitors can get intimately close to the unspoiled wilderness. Takinoya is one of 15 ryokan accommodations in the area, and it is a prestigious traditional Japanese sanctuary with more than 100 years of history.

Noboribetsu is a showcase of the tremendous forces of nature. The primeval volcanic mountains, lava pits, bubbling sulfur pools and geyser steams bursting forth from the rocky grounds of the famous Jigokudani (地獄谷 , Hell Valley) are simply breathtaking. Mythical demons known as yukijin are said to be protectors of the town — they are also, conveniently, bringers of good fortune. Visitors are greeted by huge statues of these angry-looking figures when they make their way into the town.

Once you step onto the grounds of Takinoya, the otherworldly atmosphere is swapped for a delicately tranquil ambience. The reception hall faces a Kyoto-style Japanese garden (a rarity in Hokkaido), featuring a tilting 500-year-old tree.

Guests are welcomed by staff who are dressed in exquisite traditional hakama kimonos, and led into a relaxing lounge area for welcome tea and sweets. Everyone is asked to read and sign a well-illustrated onsen etiquette guide and to acknowledge proper use of the public baths before their journey begins.

Takinoya is a family-run ryokan that has been in business since 1917. Current owner Hiderou Suga and his wife, Noriko Suga, have dedicated most of their lives to the family business. Noriko Suga is the **okami** who supervises guest services and daily operations.

THE DESIGN

Takinoya was rebuilt in 2008, and the new design fused modern Japanese aesthetics with traditional Japanese elements. Modern comforts were added to the guestrooms, and there are now also smaller rooms to accommodate solo travelers. It's interesting to note that many Japanese lodgings still do not accept or encourage solo travelers.

Rooms at Takinoya are a combination of western and Japanese style, and most rooms come with private onsen baths.

THE WATER

Not only is Noboribetsu blessed with an abundant source of hot spring water, but it also is home to nine different specific types of water. It is highly unusual for a single location to host such a large variety of waters; the town is nicknamed "Onsen Department Store" for measure. Noboribetsu was also a designated health resort town for injured soldiers during the Russo-Japanese War in the early 1900s.

At Takinoya, there are four different types of onsen water that are channeled directly to the baths from Jigokudani and other spring sources nearby — no plain water is added. Chien no Yu (地縁の湯) is a sulfur- and radium-based **rotenburo** located at the basement of the building. The sulfur content gives the water a rotten egg-like scent, but immersing yourself in the stone-lined pool of milky white water, surrounded by splendid nature, is simply delightful. The sulfuric spring is believed to help with dermatitis and chronic bronchitis; while the radium spring is said to relieve menstrual symptoms and give the immune system a boost.

The second onsen bath, Kumoi no Yu (雲井の湯), is on the top floor of the building. This is the ryokan's signature forest-facing, sodium- and iron-laced bath. The water is said to help with muscular pain and chronic eczema.

THE CUISINE

The **kaiseki** gourmet dining experience at Takinoya is one to be cherished. Etsushi Sasabuchi is the executive chef here, and he creates a sequence of meticulous courses using Hokkaido's rich produce. The meal begins with assorted cold plates of winter melon, tomato, and Hokkaido's premium Shima ebi shrimp; followed by a steaming tofu and clam broth. Next, thinly sliced hirame (flounder) sashimi from Muroran city, as well as Noboribetsu's own uni (sea urchin), are served. A choice of either Tokachigawa beef or kegani hairy crab is offered to guests — both are Hokkaido's famous delicacies.

The ryokan's signature dish of fried potato paste dumpling in a jade-green vegetable thick broth, created by Takinoya founder Otojiro Suga, is then served. The simple-looking dumpling packs quite a punch, with delicate flavors and a nice chewy texture. You can indulge in the culinary delicacies at your own pace, in private dining rooms inside the restaurant. The fare can also be enhanced by a glass of Japanese sake or western wine.

ONSEN WATER

Type: Various spring types, including Sulfur Spring; Chloride Bicarbonate Spring; Radium Spring; and Iron Spring (with sodium, aluminum, calcium and other elements)

Color and Odor: Clear; odorless

pH: 2.3 to 6.4 depending on spring type

Gensen Kakenagashi: Yes

Filtered and Circulated: No

Temperature at Source: 50°C to 64°C

Temperature at Bath: 41°C to 43°C

Takinoya
滝乃家

Address
162 Noboribetsu Onsen,
Noboribetsu, Hokkaido Prefecture,
059-0551 | +81 143-84-2222

Website
www.takinoya.co.jp

Getting Here
Convenient. Drive from New
Chitose Airport Hokkaido straight
to Takinoya (1hr). Buses are also
available from New Chitose Airport
to Noboribetsu Onsen bus station.

Rooms
High-end. Japanese and
western style.

THE TAKEAWAY

Before departing, I had a pleasant
conversation with **okami** Noriko
Suga, who usually makes her
appearance in the morning gracefully
dressed in a traditional kimono. She
told me about the interesting history
and stories of this century-old ryokan.
I really appreciate her thoughtfulness
in creating some affordable rooms for
solo travelers.

At one point, I stood and meditated
at the tilted 500-year-old tree that
still stands strong today. It was an
unforgettable experience.

Glossary

Even though not all of the terms here appear in our book, we've chosen to define the most commonly used onsen-experience-related words on these pages.

Ashiyu (足湯): Footbath.

Daiyokujo (大浴場): Public communal bathing and showering facilities inside a ryokan that are mostly gender-separated.

Datsuijo (脱衣所): Changing room. Most provide lockers or baskets to store personal belongings.

Gensen Kakenagashi (源泉掛け流し): Pure hot spring, directly from the source. No water or disinfectant added. Water is not filtered or circulated.

Geta (下駄): Traditional Japanese sandals, typically made from wood and with a fabric thong; usually worn with a yukata. Some ryokan lodgings provide geta sandals to be worn outside the building.

Hito (秘湯): A secluded onsen, usually situated in a hidden location.

Insen (飲泉): Potable hot spring water. The Japanese believe that certain types of hot spring water contain ingredients that are beneficial to the body.

Irori (囲炉裏): A sunken hearth. Traditional Japanese-style fireplace that is built into the floor; used for cooking or heating.

Jifunsen (自噴泉): An artesian spring that gushes out of the earth's cracks due to natural pressures. This type of spring is extremely rare in Japan and only makes up 1 percent of all hot springs in the country.

Kaiseki (懐石／会席): A traditional Japanese mutli-course meal served in a specific sequence, from appetizer to dessert. A typical type of meal that is served in a traditional Japanese ryokan.

Kashikiriburo (貸切風呂): Private onsen baths that can be reserved in advance.

Konyoku (混浴): Mixed-gender bath.

Kotatsu (こたつ): A low, heated wooden table covered by a blanket. Legs can be placed under the table to keep them warm during winter. It is commonly used in Japanese homes and traditional ryokan lodgings.

Nabe (鍋): A pot usually made from ceramic, used for cooking and hot pot.

Nihonshu (日本酒): Japanese rice wine, more commonly known as Japanese sake outside of Japan.

Nyuto Tegata (入湯手形): An onsen-hopping pass. A day pass to visit several onsen baths at a discounted price.

Obi (帯): A belt made of fabric, used to fasten a kimono or yukata.

Okami (女将): Chief female service manager of a traditional Japanese ryokan; one who is in charge of guest services and operations. The role is usually taken up by the wife or a family member of the owner, and is passed from one generation to the next.

Onnayu (女湯): Women's bath.

Onsen (温泉): Hot spring.

Otokoyu (男湯): Men's bath.

Rotenburo (露天風呂): An open-air onsen bath.

Ryokan (旅館): Traditional Japanese inn.

Shabu Shabu (しゃぶしゃぶ): Japanese-style hot pot, using clear water or dashi broth to cook meat and vegetables in a pot.

Tatami (畳): A straw-woven mat used as flooring material in a traditional Japanese house or ryokan. The size of the guest rooms in a ryokan is usually measured by the number of mats. Each mat comes in a standard size of 91cm by 182cm.

Toji (湯治): Hot spring therapy. The Japanese believe in spending days or weeks at an onsen with alleged medicinal properties to try to cure an illness, rehabilitate, or simply rest and recuperate.

Uchiburo (内風呂): Indoor onsen bath.

Washi (和紙): Traditional handmade Japanese paper made from tree bark fibers. It is a common material used in wooden sliding screen doors (aka shoji) found in traditional Japanese ryokan lodgings.

Washitsu (和室): Traditional Japanese-style room, usually with tatami floors.

Wayoshitsu (和洋室): A room with both Japanese- and western-style elements. Usually with tatami floors and western-style beds.

Yatenburo (野天風呂): A natural open-air onsen pool, found in the wilderness.

Yoshitsu (洋室): Western-style room.

Yu (ゆ / 湯): Hot water, also referred to as bathwater.

Yuba (湯葉): Layers of tofu skin made from thick soy milk.

Yukata (浴衣): A kimono-like robe made from cotton, fastened with an obi belt around the waist. It is a typical garment provided by the ryokan that can be worn inside the premises. People strolling around in yukata garments is a common sight in some onsen towns.

Yunohana (湯の花): Natural deposits in the hot spring water that have been formed as a result of minerals being crystallized after being exposed to oxygen.

References

By Author

1. Neff, Robert. Japan's Hidden Hot Springs. Rutland, Vermont: Charles E. Tuttle Co., 1995. Print.

2. Brue, Alexia. Cathedrals of the Flesh: My Search for the Perfect Bath. London: Bloomsbury, 2010. Print.

3. Talmadge, Eric. Getting Wet: Adventures in the Japanese Bath. Tokyo; New York: Kodansha International, 2006. Print.

By Title

4. Sacred Waters: A Guide to Japanese Hot Springs. Annette Masai, August Ericsson. Sweden: Votum & Gullers Förlag, 2014. Print.

5. The Japanese Bath. Bruce Smith, Yoshiko Yamamoto. Salt Lake City: Gibbs Smith Publisher, 2001. Print.

6. Ryokan: Japan's Finest Spas and Inns. Akihito Seki, Elizabeth Heilman Brooke. Boston: Tuttle Publishing, 2012. Print.

7. Japanese Inns and Hot Springs: A Guide to Japan's Best Ryokan & Onsen. Rob Goss, Seki Akihito. Tokyo; Rutland Vermont; Singapore: Tuttle Publishing, 2017. Print.

8. Warming & Relaxing: 16 Hot Springs You Should Visit in Japan. Tokyo: Nippan Ips Co., 2017. Print.

9. 宿の主人が語る 究極の癒やし湯 Seeker of Warmth 540 号 . 東京：八重州出版，2017. Print.

10. 一度は入りたい秘湯・古湯 100 選 . 東京： 交通新聞社 , Kotsushinbunsha, 2017. Print.

11. ぶくぶく自噴泉めぐり . 篠遠 泉 , 長岡 努 , 永瀬 美佳 . 東京：山と渓谷社 . 2017. Print.

12. 温泉―自然と文化 Hot Spring ― Nature and Culture. 東京：日本温泉協会 . 2006. Print.

13. Discover Japan (ディスカバージャパン) 2019 年 2 月号 雑誌 . Tokyo: Discover Japan Inc, 2019. Print.

Websites

14. www.hitou.or.jp

15. spa-misasa.jp/japan-heritage/en/bathing-method/

16. www.spa.or.jp

17. www.jph-ri.or.jp

18. www.japantimes.co.jp/life/2010/10/28/people/ryokan-owner-kazushi-sato/

19. www.projectdesign.jp/201409/pn-akita/001582.php

20. yamagata-np.jp/feature/kankohukko/kj_2014040100017.php

21. visitkinosaki.com/in-the-area/kinosaki-onsen/about-kinosaki-onsen/

22. www.shirahone.org/

23. koboku.org/articles/97

24. serai.jp/hobby/172526

25. ancient-japan-izumo.com

26. www.izm.ed.jp/english/

About the Author

Iris Law is an avid traveler, and her destination of choice is Japan. Her adventures in the country began in 1998, when she made her first trip to Tokyo. She gradually started to explore areas outside of the big cities, including the countryside, where most hot spring resorts are located. Her first onsen bath took place in Noboribetsu, Hokkaido, in 2002. Since then, she has visited more than 100 onsen ryokan accommodations in Japan.

Iris was born in Hong Kong and grew up in Toronto. She is currently living in Hong Kong.

Man Mo Media

Author: Iris Law

Editor: Adele Wong

Creative Director: Mike Hung

Illustrator: Neri Ishida

Photographers: Iris Law, Gallant Nien

First Published: Hong Kong 2020
ISBN 978-988-77560-2-6

ManMoMedia

manmomedia.com